AFTER
THIS LIFE

AFTER THIS LIFE

*What Catholics Believe
About What Happens Next*

FR. BENEDICT J. GROESCHEL, C.F.R.

Our Sunday Visitor Publishing Division
Our Sunday Visitor, Inc.
Huntington, Indiana 46750

Nihil Obstat
Reverend Michael Heintz, Ph.D.
Censor Librorum

Imprimatur
✠ John M. D'Arcy
Bishop of Fort Wayne–South Bend
August 17, 2009

Every reasonable effort has been made to determine copyright holders of excerpted materials and to secure permissions as needed. If any copyrighted materials have been inadvertently used in this work without proper credit being given in one form or another, please notify Our Sunday Visitor in writing so that future printings of this work may be corrected accordingly.

Our Sunday Visitor Publishing Division
Our Sunday Visitor, Inc.
200 Noll Plaza
Huntington, IN 46750

1-800-348-2440
bookpermissions@osv.com

ISBN: 978-1-59276-442-6 (Inventory No. T679)
LCCN: 2009936134

Cover design: Lindsey Luken
Cover art: The Crosiers
Interior design by Sherri L. Hoffman

PRINTED IN THE UNITED STATES OF AMERICA

To all beloved friends who have passed beyond this life.

Contents

ACKNOWLEDGMENTS

I am very grateful to John Collins, my faithful editor. Over the past couple of years I have been struggling with physical problems and especially the effects of a stroke that I experienced about three months before I finished this book. It is only because of the help and encouragement of John that I have been able to bring this book to its conclusion. It concerns a topic that I believe is extremely important to many people, including me, people who are growing old or struggling with infirmities. It is for these people especially that I have written *After This Life*.

I also thank Father Patrick Fitzsimons for his comments on early versions of this book, and I especially thank Father Joseph O'Hara, whose generous help was instrumental in preparing the final manuscript for publication.

As always, I am very grateful to Bert Ghezzi of Our Sunday Visitor for his continued encouragement on this book and over the years.

I hope many will find this book a personal help. I write my books as a form of spiritual direction, and I only ask the Holy Spirit that my books may be a blessing and a help to those who read them.

FATHER BENEDICT
The Solemnity of the Assumption
August 15, 2009

INTRODUCTION

"In my end is my beginning."

T. S. ELIOT (FROM "FOUR QUARTETS")

The end of this life and the afterlife that follows have always been among the most important concerns of human beings. We see evidence of this interest in the oldest ruins of human civilization, the dolmans or tombs of County Clare in Ireland. These are incredible uncut stone structures that required the lifting of ledges weighing one hundred thousand pounds, fifteen thousand years ago. We see such evidence as well in the oldest intact human structures, the Egyptian pyramids, which are profound testimonies to the importance of the concern about life after death to people who lived thousands of years ago. This concern was so great among the Egyptians that it actually overshadowed the importance of the present life. Virtually every ancient culture we know of paid great attention to the death of its members, surrounding their passing with ritual and ceremony, with prayers and magical rites. The universality of such burial rites and tombs, therefore, raises the question: Why was it so important to build a house for the dead unless one thought that in some mysterious way they would need it in some kind of continued existence?

In many ways we are far removed from our ancient ancestors, yet the funerals of those we love and of our public figures are no less important or ritualistic to us. We lay our dead as lovingly in their graves or in their mausoleums as did our ancestors. We visit our cemeteries, and at the graves of our loved ones we feel less alone. At these moments, no matter what our religious convictions, we are left with the inescapable feeling that death is not the end it seems to be, that somehow there is something more. Even beyond this is the experience of many who are aware that they are approaching the end of life from illness or advanced age. Death is drawing near, but the feeling remains that death may not really be final. We are reminded of the haunting and perceptive words of the great Christian poet T. S. Elliot, "In my end is my beginning," and we hope.

What actually happens at the moment of bodily death and after becomes of overwhelming importance to us all when a dear relative or friend dies. The question that haunts our minds, that cannot be put aside, is: Will I ever see my loved one again? Even the agnostics and atheists among us have trouble freeing themselves of this question.

Having looked death in the eye more than once and having for all intents and purposes been dead with no vital signs for half an hour, I feel obligated to write this book, not only to help others deal with death, but to explain, as well, what the Christian faith and the teaching of the Church tell us about the afterlife; that is, about what comes next.

Almost forty years of working as a psychologist have taught me that the most common personal problem of sane people is anxiety and fear. Someone has perceptively written: "We are afraid to live and afraid to die." And this is the truth — often we lead partial lives, afraid to take risks, afraid to live fully. We are too timid, too unsure, to fully commit ourselves in faith and trust to God and in love to other people as we spend our brief "day on earth." Simultaneously, we do all we can to avoid the plain fact that we are mortal — that death is our lot, our inevitable future. In denial we try to go on, living day after day, oblivious of the fact that we and those we care for will one day die. We live as if the world were static, yet it changes constantly; every microsecond brings enormous change. We pretend that it is not the nature of all life to be born, to grow, to decline, and eventually to perish. Thus, when life-threatening events occur, many of us are very ill-prepared to face them, and when we look in desperation to friends for help, we are shocked to discover that these people are unable to deal with the possibility of death either — unable to help us when we need them most.

We Live in a Culture That Denies Death

The denial of death is one of the primary characteristics of our contemporary culture. The writer Susan Sontag, a keen observer of our modern world, saw this clearly. Although not religious herself, and certainly no friend of the Church, she was perceptive enough to write: "For those who live neither with religious consolations about death nor with a sense of death (or of anything else) as natural, death is the obscene mystery, the ultimate affront, the thing that cannot be controlled. It can only be denied."[1]

Wherever we look we find evidence of this: Our drugstore and supermarket shelves are crowded with products designed to make us look younger. People spend incredible amounts of money on cosmetics, hair dyes, hair replacements, and a thousand other things, all in an effort to pretend that they are not aging, to deny the fact that their physical bodies are coming closer to death with every passing second. Large numbers of people willingly — even enthusiastically — submit to unneeded and potentially dangerous plastic surgeries, not to improve their health or to cure some disease, but simply to pretend to be younger, to deny that they must someday experience physical death. Sometimes even our doctors encourage this way of thinking, telling us that every ailment has a cure — that death can be postponed forever.

The frantic denial of death in our culture has reached the point where it has become a sad joke. I read not too long ago a description of something called the Lifespan Extending Villa,[2] a house designed by two architects named Arakawa and Gins. The house is in East Hampton, Long Island, a wealthy seaside community. It is, however, not your typical summer house — even for the well-to-do. It features an uneven and bumpy concrete floor descending toward a sunken kitchen; walls painted in forty colors; multiple levels and windows at varying heights; and light switches and outlets where one would least expect them. The basic idea is to remove the comforts of home, because comfort leads to complacency and this — according to the architects — leads to aging, and aging leads to death. "It's immoral," Gins declares, "that people have to die." These two claim to have spent the last forty years "studying how architecture might best be used to sustain life," and they state in their website that their goal is to give us the "power to go on indefinitely." This house of theirs is a pathetic attempt at immortality, their desperate attempt to pretend we do not have to die.

Even when death finally comes — as it inevitably must — we still do not stop denying it. This denial actually invades the funeral itself. How often at a wake do we hear bizarre and unintentionally ghoulish remarks such as: "Didn't they do a nice job on him? He looks great." That's usually because no one ever saw him wearing a suit and tie before or holding the Rosary in his hand. He — the deceased — actually looks terrible, and he's going to look a lot worse in a couple of weeks. But these are things we don't want to accept, things we can't even force ourselves to face. In fact we work very hard at not facing them. Cremation used to be so unusual that one had to request it in a legal document before death or it would not be performed. Now cremation is commonplace. There are many reasons for this, and some of them are certainly understandable. However, one of the reasons for the incredible increase in the occurrence of cremation is that this practice enables us to pretend that death has not occurred. Confronted with the body of the deceased at a wake, we are psychologically forced to acknowledge that person's death. However, if all we see is an elegant, decorative urn, one that seems to have no relationship to a human body, we are given an out. We heave a sigh of relief, for that person's death can remain forever unreal to us.

I think of this frightened, childish view of things and cannot help but compare it to the vision the Church gives us of death, one in which fear is replaced by hope, one in which physical death has lost its sting through Christ, the One who opens up eternal life to us. In the great poem "The Canticle of the Sun," which is attributed to Saint Francis of Assisi, all of God's creation is presented to us. We are introduced to the sun and the moon, the wind, water, and fire. Each one of them is called our brother or sister, and Saint Francis praises God for the creation of every one of them. At the end of the poem we are introduced to a character who, from our contemporary point of view, is unexpected and startling in this great hymn to creation. To Saint Francis, however, the praising of God for the existence of "Sister Bodily Death" must have seemed the most natural thing in the world:

> Be thou praised, O Lord, for our Sister Bodily Death,
> From whom no man living may escape.
> Woe to those who die in mortal sin.
> Blessed are they who shall be found doing Thy most
>   Holy Will,
> For the second dying shall work them no evil.[3]

Here we see that it is sin, not death, that is to be feared; that physical death for the devout Christian is an inevitable part of life, one that should hold no terror for us because it has become an element of God's great work of redemption. Through the Resurrection of Christ, bodily death is irrevocably defeated, transformed from our destroyer into our sister, our friend who embraces us gently and opens for us the pathway to a life in which no harm can ever again befall us.

What I hope to do in this book is to bring out in a calm and meaningful way what our faith and the New Testament tell us of our "Sister Bodily Death" and of life after death. There is great hope here, a hope that should help us to become more realistic about our lives and our eventual deaths. You may find these truths most consoling and uplifting. Next we will look at the tradition of the Church, what saints and great Christians have told us over the last two thousand years. You might be surprised by how much we know about the goodness and mercy of God, and this may help you when you ask the question: What happens next? We must remember that what we believe happens next is very much going to define what is happening to us right now.

We should never approach a question of this importance without prayer. In fact, in prayer alone will we find our way into the contemplation of the mystery we call life and its twin, the mystery we call death. Only prayer can help us to comprehend the answers to our questions. Our prayers should, first of all, be to Christ, our Savior, whose most important words are words that brim with hope: "Let not your hearts be troubled; believe in God, believe also in me. In my Father's house are many rooms.... I go and prepare a place for you" (John 14:1-2, 3).

Someone recently gave me at Christmas a beautiful book by Nicolas Cheetham called *Universe: A Journey from Earth to the Edge of the Cosmos.* This is because I love to read about astronomy from a religious and meditative point of view. *Universe: A Journey from Earth to the Edge of the Cosmos* shows the incredible power and immensity of God made manifest in the universe. The book you are holding in your hands is *not* going to be a journey through the cosmos. It will instead be a journey beyond the cosmos, beyond the material world, where souls live on even as the body decomposes and disappears; where human beings retain their identities and the ability to do many things that are not related to physical actions; where the good, the just, the saved await the end of the world, the Last Judgment, the final establishment of the Kingdom of God, and eternal life.

This is the most important thing in your life and in mine. Where will we be and where will those dear to us be in that reality beyond this world of limited time and space? Every thinking believer ought to be interested and even deeply concerned about what happens to us next. In His parables, our blessed Savior very frequently spoke of death and the Last Judgment, warning people to be ready, to be prepared. I hope this book will help you as you prepare yourself for that inevitability, that reality which is so much more profound than the passing shadow we call our life here on earth, that reality for which we have all been made.

The Promise of Life to Come

When I first contemplated writing this book, I toyed with the idea of calling it *After This Our Exile.* As most Catholics will readily recognize, those are words taken from the exquisitely beautiful prayer to Our Lady, the "*Salve, Regina*" or, in English, the "Hail, Holy Queen." This prayer was composed by a blind and crippled monk, Blessed Herman of Richenau, a thousand years ago. As is so often the case for people with severe physical problems, life was very difficult for him. This led him to see more clearly than most that his life was an exile from his real home with our heavenly

Father, Christ, the Virgin Mary, and the saints. What person reading these pages has not at some point felt that the burdens of life were simply too heavy to bear, that these burdens overwhelmed and blotted out any satisfaction, any joy that this time on earth could bring? Blessed Herman felt this way often, and the only thing that kept him going was the certitude that the life he was living was not the only thing that God had in store for him — that his exile was temporary, and he would one day go home.

At times I feel this way myself. The effects of my accident of several years ago still linger, making many tasks that once were simple very difficult. I have recently suffered a small stroke. It is nothing compared with what many people must endure, and my doctors assure me I will recover completely, yet it makes me very aware of new and annoying limitations, of the fact that physical life itself is limited and sometimes exhausting. I pray the "*Salve Regina*" often. It helps me greatly to remember these words composed by Blessed Herman, to recall that my present life, my exile from God, is temporary, a mere prelude to a life more wonderful and more vibrant than any of us can imagine.

At least some of those who read this book will have suffered tragedies or catastrophes causing them to think that they would rather be dead than continue living. Every thinking person knows that in the midst of terrible tragedy, anyone can be brought to a moment of wishing that life would end. This life on earth can have moments of exquisite beauty, of great satisfaction, but it can also be a "valley of tears." We all know that happiness can be transformed into sorrow in the space of a few minutes. The news of some great personal loss or illness can make all the difference. We should also all be aware that no earthly tragedy is final, that our heavenly Father yearns for our salvation, that Jesus has gone "to make a place" for us, a place of joy beyond all sadness, beyond all exile.

A vital awareness of the promise of the life to come, the life that the Son of God won for us by His holy life, terrible death, and glorious Resurrection fills us with hope and strength in facing this life and its inevitable challenges — in looking forward with courage and in hope to what comes next.

Rendering an Account to Our Maker

There is, however, yet another reason for thinking as clearly as possible about life after death: so that we may prepare each day to give an account to our Maker of how we have spent our lives, how we have treated others, and how we have observed His commandments. Our Savior tells us that everyone will be rewarded according to his deeds (Matthew 16:27). The constant message of sacred Scripture and especially of Jesus Christ's preaching is that we must be constantly ready because He comes at a time we least expect.

The world tells us that our lives are our own and can be used as we see fit. With reflection we can see something quite different: that our lives are a gift from God, and one day we will surrender them back to our heavenly Father. At every moment of our time on earth God has expectations of us. He has made us in His divine image, and He calls us to reflect this image by serving in charity. This draws us out of ourselves, inspiring us to spend ourselves for others as Jesus did. The daunting yet liberating standard that God gives us, the example of what a human life can and should be, is Jesus. Obviously none of us can live up to such a standard completely, but we must do our best, and we must strive for this consistently, for — like it or not — God will finally judge us by this standard.

Helping Others toward Salvation

Another reason for thinking about life and death is that we are responsible for helping others on their way to salvation. Consequently, the good Christian should, by words, deeds, and actions, be an appropriate witness to the fact that we shall all be judged. With all this in mind, we shall soon begin our meditation on what are called the last things: death, judgment, Hell, and Heaven, as well as the transient state of purification we call Purgatory.

Many people have written in this vein over the centuries. Generally speaking, such writings attempt to be very objective, telling us what to expect. This is, of course, quite helpful, but what I hope to do in this book is to focus on what we think and feel about these realities as we make our way toward them. What does death mean to you now, or judgment, or the different possibilities of the realities of your life after death? I do not intend to focus much attention on Hell, although it is obviously very important. What needs to be said can be said briefly because I have some knowledge of the kind of people who read my books. I can't say that they look to me or to anyone else like those on their way to Hell. In modern times we have seen people — despots, vicious criminals, and others — who appear to be headed for eternal damnation. The kind of people who read this book are entirely different from the sadists and great murderers of modern history. While the Church never identifies someone as being in Hell, anyone who lived during the latter part of the twentieth century knows there are people whom one would not be particularly surprised to find there. So we will leave Hell to a very brief consideration and spend a good deal of our time in trying to learn what the Catholic tradition says concerning that mysterious interim period called Purgatory and also about Heaven. Most people think that you can know almost nothing about Heaven; but, as you will see, that is not entirely true.

Each of the realities of the passing into eternity needs to be explored carefully. If you slowly contemplate these considerations, which I have gathered from my own meditations and readings, I believe you may find them helpful. Of course, I must leave some questions unanswered and even more answers incomplete, but I am trying to help as many sincere Christians — Catholics, Protestant, and Orthodox — as possible. Having lived almost eighty years and having been blessed with a firm faith over the decades, despite my failures and shortcomings (and perhaps even because of them) I am inescapably faced with the question: What comes next? If you are interested, then this book is for you. We have a fascinating journey beyond the cosmos ahead of us. Don't forget to approach it with prayer.

Chapter One

BODILY DEATH

"Lord, for your faithful people life is changed, not ended."

THE MASS FOR THE DEAD[4]

Through the centuries, believing Christians have thought, prayed, and spoken about the end of earthly life and what follows. Although various lists have been proposed, for as complete a consideration as possible we are going to explore five realities: death, judgment, Hell, Purgatory, and the eternal life that we call Heaven. By definition, all of these realities lie beyond ordinary human perception; they elude our complete understanding. They are mysteries; in fact, all that attends death is a mystery. We perceive the biological processes leading up to death, for these are tangible and measurable, but the actual experience of death lies in another domain of being, one that is mysterious, as are the judgment of God, eternal loss, purification, and eternal life.

Before proceeding further we must make sure that we have an appreciation of mystery, for our journey will be through very mysterious territory. Not only is mystery an awareness of that which we don't fully comprehend, but in the sense in which we are using the word, we can define "mystery" as the deliberate acceptance of the fact that much exists that surpasses human understanding and experience. When one considers the limitations of the human mind, one realizes that the need to accept and appreciate mystery is profound. Sacred Scripture and sound theology provide some insight into mystery. Our Savior spoke of the "secrets of the kingdom of heaven" (Matthew 13:11), and Saint Paul, in one of his most eloquent passages says, "O the depth of the riches and wisdom and knowledge of God! How unsearchable are his judgments and how inscrutable his ways!" (Romans 11:33).

In Ephesians 3, Saint Paul speaks several times of the mystery of Christ, which had been revealed to him and which he shares with those to whom he is writing.

The Fathers of the Church without exception see the mysterious as contained within the revealed truths of faith. Saint Augustine, a man of immense human intelligence and gifts, particularly reminds us of the limitations of what we can know.

From a purely human point of view, Albert Einstein — considered by most people to be the greatest scientific mind of our time — said that someone without a sense of mystery might as well be dead. This most brilliant man was absolutely convinced of the great limitations of what the human mind can comprehend and equally convinced of realities far beyond that which reason could reveal to us. Although some still claim that he was an atheist, he was not. His writings show a great sensitivity to what we might call the religious dimension of existence. Writing of God (a word he never hesitated to use), he stated: "The deeply emotional conviction of the presence of a superior reasoning power, which is revealed in the incomprehensible universe, forms my idea of God."[5] And speaking directly of faith and religion, he said: "My religion is a humble admiration of the illimitable superior spirit who reveals himself in the slight details we are able to perceive with our frail and feeble minds."[6]

We will, one by one, try to explore what we can understand or legitimately speculate about these most important realities, acknowledging that even shreds of knowledge of transcendent reality are infinitely precious. Because we must rely on divine revelation and sacred Scripture far more than on what our "frail and feeble minds" are able to tell us, we must proceed carefully and reverently; the saints, as always, will help us as we go along.

"Death Be Not Proud"

These words, quoted from the great sonnet of John Donne,[7] the English poet, have been recognized as part of an immensely powerful statement about death. At the end of his poem Donne writes: "Death, thou shalt die," and this has always been the Christian conviction. As we approach the question of death, it is vital to keep this in mind and be aware that whatever we say has been overwhelmed and transcended by the grace of Christ and His Resurrection and promise of eternal life.

For the Christian, death is never an end, for God has not made us to end. Death for us is infinitely more than the cessation of biological life, which is what it is for animals. Animals can be considered animated bodies: Full of feelings, emotions, and impulses, they have been given life by God, but they have not been made in the divine image and likeness as we have been. Therefore, they do not possess immortal souls. The angels, on the other hand, are pure spirit; not being material beings, they do not know any kind of death, and they are unchanged by time. Humankind, however, stands between the two as the only part of God's creation that is part of the passing physical world and the eternal spiritual one. We are a joining of body and immortal soul, although this union has been an imperfect and uneasy one since the moment sin entered human life. Our emotions and passions often rule us as they rule animals, yet we are capable of astounding spiritual depth. To us, physical death is inevitable, but for us death is a separation rather than an ending, a separation that will eventually be healed by the grace of God. We must never forget that our death has been conquered in the Resurrection of Christ. Although physical death is our fate and may indeed be wrenching and horribly painful, it is never final. At the end of time our souls will be reunited with our glorified and resurrected bodies in a union — a wholeness — far more perfect than we presently have the capacity to imagine.

But what is death really? Saint Paul clearly teaches that death came into the world through Original Sin. Does this mean that if there never had been the mysterious Fall of man, there would never be the cessation of biological life? To us, whose only experience is that of a sinful world, this seems to be an absurdity, bringing to mind a world in which no one passed from this life and in which everything became more and more crowded and even more tedious than it already is. We have, however, lost the ability to conceive of what life undamaged by sin might actually be, what a life untouched by death might mean. Death in the sense that Saint Paul uses the word, therefore, is mysterious, something we cannot yet imagine.

As we know it, death is almost always a cause of sorrow, grief, and even horror. Even great faith does not enable us to ignore our emotions, nor does it make us impervious to loss. Some of the great saints were overcome with grief when confronted by the deaths of those they loved. Jesus wept at the tomb of His friend Lazarus. We are, however, occasionally given the grace to experience death somewhat differently. Sometimes death's sorrow is muted for us, and the joy of a holy soul returning home to God becomes at least somewhat apparent. The passing of an elderly, devout, and holy person is often not experienced in a tragic way. I have attended the funerals of such people, and they were celebrations of victory, recognitions of the passing of a very good person. Grief was present, of course, but it was overshadowed by the knowledge that that person had gone on to a well-deserved reward, that the earthly trials of such a person had ended, to be replaced by joy and contentment. At such a funeral one could easily sing the words of Saint Paul: "O death, where is thy victory? O death, where is thy sting?" (1 Corinthians 15:55).

The Experience of Another's Death

On some level we all know death to be part of the experience of life, but few give it much thought at all. Comprehension of death is something we are not born with but acquire. Small children have no understanding of it; they cannot even begin to understand that they will not go on forever, and when they are confronted with the death of a family member, they usually think that person has gone away and will one day return. Children usually first encounter death, however, when a canary or a gerbil or even the family dog dies. I can recall digging up my pet canary a week after it died when I was a small boy and being shocked by the worms and the decay. I wondered if the same thing was happening to my grandfather who had recently died and was buried in a beautiful cemetery not far away. The real meaning of death, the psychological impact of it, however, was diminished for me and most children of the modern age because we often experienced unreal death in films or the media, something that is even truer among the young of today. At the movies, sitting in a darkened theater, I often witnessed dramas that evoked feelings of sadness, loss, or sorrow. As soon as I got into the bright sunlight outside, however, all that was left behind. I knew that I would soon be able to see my favorite actor in his next film despite the fact that I had just lamented his death in this one. Such things cannot help but affect the way young people perceive death, making it less and less real, less and less comprehensible for them.

In late childhood or perhaps in the early teens the reality of death, along with its finality and often its sorrow or tragedy, finally begins to dawn on us. You may have noticed this if you have encountered one of those rare occasions in which a student in junior or senior high school dies. The other students appear to be dazed, almost helpless. They seem to think they have witnessed the impossible, not understanding the commonplaceness of death, still not fully grasping that it is something we all must experience. The superficial bravado that characterizes the class leaders evaporates into stunned silence. They look desperately to others — especially to religious people — to help them. Even the teenaged skeptic appears to be stunned and mystified by the finality, the immensity, the mystery of death.

The effects that the death of another will have on us are often unpredictable. Sometimes we stand emotionless before the open casket of someone we loved deeply, unable to feel sorrow, unable to feel anything. At other times we are surprised to find ourselves reacting strongly to the death of someone we didn't even know, perhaps someone we admired but had never met. I will never forget the weekend that started with the announcement that President Kennedy had been shot and killed. Even his critics and political foes sat by the television all weekend and grieved over the death of this vital young man. I have seen this happen other times as well. The outpouring of grief when Princess Diana was tragically killed seemed unreasonable, almost bizarre. People throughout the world who had never even seen her or given much thought to the British monarchy broke into uncontrollable sobs. It is inexplicable, but something about her life and death touched people profoundly.

Death can come gently to carry off loved ones, as it often does with the passing of an elderly person; it can also come tragically with an accident or illness involving a young life. No matter how death comes, it comes with the same questions: Will I ever see my loved one again? Will death be the final end that it appears to be?

Faced with death, the vast majority of human beings turn to hope in God. This happens even to people who have hardly thought of God at any point during their lives. I recall that the wife of a president of the Soviet Union, an official atheist, made the Sign of the Cross over his casket as it was placed into the Kremlin wall for the entire world to see on television. I went a few years ago to a non-religious funeral where everyone was expected to say something complimentary about the deceased but no one prayed. In the two or three minutes allotted to each speaker, all but two of the mourners expressed some kind of belief in God and in an afterlife. I was asked to lead all in prayer. One of the mourners, however, a distinguished professor under whom I had studied decades before, did not mention God or the afterlife in his eulogy. After it was over he apologized, saying that he had been raised without any religion. Nonetheless, he later revealed that he had wanted to speak of God but had not done so, fearing he might say something that would be offensive. In those words I heard an atheist apologize for his atheism. God can do many unexpected things.

Death is especially frightening because it is the end of all that is familiar to us. To the unbeliever it is a journey into nothingness. To the believer it represents the passage into a different and splendid domain of being. Sacred Scripture tells us many mysterious things about that domain, which we will examine in this book. One of the most important of these mysteries is that we are to have an existence without time or the other dimensions of the reality with which we are familiar, making us think of the famous quotation from the Second Letter of Saint Peter, "... with the Lord... a thousand years as one day" (2 Peter 3:8).

Beyond this is the mystery of functioning without our physical bodies, of being able to perceive without the senses, of knowing in some other way who we are and who others are without being able to hear or see or touch them. These are mysteries that a clergyman is often asked about, and they are questions he can never adequately answer. Obviously, all of this is deeply shrouded in mystery, a mystery that cannot be penetrated completely by the human mind.

Nonetheless, the Bible clearly presents people coming back from the grave and just as clearly being able to communicate with those who are living in this world. There are a number of examples of this in sacred Scripture, but perhaps the most intriguing one is the event we call the Transfiguration. Here we encounter a powerfully dramatic scene in which the Apostles actually see Christ speaking with Moses and the Prophet Elijah.

There are, of course, the many appearances of Christ after His death — to Mary Magdalene, to the Apostles, and at one time to five hundred people, an event that unfortunately is not described in any detail. Down through the history of the Church there are many examples of Christ, His Mother, or some saint appearing to a devout and holy person. These apparitions are part of the Catholic and Orthodox traditions. They are rarely challenged except by complete skeptics who challenge everything. The general assumption is that if people live on after death in some way we don't understand, there is consequently no reason to question the possibility that they will communicate with us.

Encountering the Dead

Along with the fascinating and mysterious apparitions after death of Christ and His Blessed Mother, there are the repeated experiences of people who sincerely believe they have in one way or another encountered one of their dear ones who are deceased. While it is very easy to dismiss these accounts as wishful thinking or psychological illusion arising out of grief, there are so many such accounts and they are so varied that one must at least pause and consider them. On three occasions in my life, such things have occurred to me. I know definitely that I did not see, touch, or perceive with the senses any person from the afterlife, but in a startling way I knew they were there. One case particularly struck me, that of a young man who had taken his own life, a very troubled but intelligent young man who was grieving over getting a "Dear John" letter from his girlfriend. While I was praying at Mass a few days after his funeral, it suddenly became clear to me that he was there. I saw nothing, but I was startled by the realization that he was a changed person: He was at peace. The awareness was so clear and startling that I paused in the prayers and looked up at the doorway where he actually seemed to be standing.

Obviously, there is no way to prove such an experience or to disprove it. *A priori* a person can deny such a possibility, but I do not accept all *a priori* judgments when they relate to what goes beyond this world. Such judgments completely ignore facts concerning the many different kinds of people who report experiences of the presence of the dead; they assume knowledge that no human can possess. It simply seems to me that such experiences are somehow similar to encountering a person in life, and yet they are simultaneously profoundly different from such encounters. They are encounters with a person who is beyond this world. The truth is that I was shocked and grieved by this young man's death, and it is certainly true that I may have been reacting to that grief. The experience, itself, however, remains clear in my mind, and it gives me reason to understand how others have experienced the presence of a loved one who has gone before them. I would be the last person in the world to simply dismiss this *a priori* in the name of psychology. I am reminded of a quotation from *Markings*, the deeply spiritual book written by Dag Hammarskjöld, Secretary General of the United Nations: "My friend the psychologist has understood nothing."[8] In all my use of psychology in my work and my understanding of life I always keep that observation of Hammarskjöld in mind. He puts things into a cautious perspective.

Chapter Two

JUDGMENT AFTER DEATH

"True and just are thy judgments."

APOCALYPSE 16:7 (ALSO KNOWN AS REVELATION)

The Inevitability of Judgment and the Journey to God

Throughout human history there has been an almost universal recognition that at the end of life we all render some kind of an account of our lives to God. Even when the understanding of the one God is clouded and confused, human beings in almost every culture have a strong sense that they will be judged by their Maker in some way after death. In the Greco-Roman pagan world even little children were buried with miniature scales of justice in their hands, just as adults were. Almost all ancient people, including the Jews, prayed for the dead or had rituals of atonement for their sins so that their deceased loved ones would be able to obtain a favorable judgment. We see this very clearly in the Second Book of Maccabees. In this Old Testament book, the general, Judas, orders that prayers be offered for his dead soldiers so that they may be released from their sins:

> ... Judas and his men went to take up the bodies of the fallen and to bring them back to lie with their kinsmen in the sepulchres of their fathers. Then under the tunic of every one of the dead they found sacred tokens of the idols of Jamnia, which the law forbids the Jews to wear. And it became clear to all that this was why these men had fallen. So they all blessed the ways of the Lord, the righteous Judge, who reveals the things that are hidden; and they turned to prayer, beseeching that the sin which had been committed might be wholly blotted out. And the noble Judas exhorted the

people to keep themselves free from sin, for they had seen with their own eyes what had happened because of the sin of those who had fallen. He also took up a collection, man by man... and sent it to Jerusalem to provide for a sin offering. In doing this he acted very well and honorably, taking account of the resurrection. For if he were not expecting that those who had fallen would rise again, it would have been superfluous and foolish to pray for the dead. (2 Maccabees 12:39-44)

This is a truly remarkable passage. For the Jew of the Old Testament no less than the Jews of today, idolatry is the great sin, the one least deserving of forgiveness. There can be no question but that those soldiers who died with "sacred tokens of the idols" on their persons were guilty of an immense transgression. Yet here we see Judas and his men hopeful that God would forgive their dead comrades — that their sin would be "wholly blotted out" — purely as a result of their prayers and offerings.

At the conclusion of this chapter the biblical writer says about Judas and his actions for his fallen comrades: "Therefore he made atonement for the dead, that they might be delivered from their sin" (2 Maccabees 12:45). What greater assertion concerning the efficacy of prayers for the dead could there possibly be than the scriptural assurance that Judas's prayers and sacrifices were actually considered an atonement, an atonement for sins committed by those who were now dead?

This belief that the dead undergo judgment and can benefit from the prayers of the living continues in Judaism through the present time, although many people somehow deny this. The famous prayer called the "Kaddish"[9] has been part of Jewish life for untold centuries. It extols the infinite greatness of God and speaks of man's acceptance of God's often inscrutable will. Early on, this prayer became one said by mourners as they tried to come to terms with the loss they had undergone. Eventually the recitation of this prayer in memory of the dead became a universal custom (although there is no mention of death in it), and it was generally believed to help ease the trials and sufferings of the souls of the deceased as they made their way from *Gehenna* (a place of either torment or purification for the dead — Purgatory) to *Gan Eden* (Paradise), a journey that in Jewish tradition can take up to a full year after death depending on the sins of the deceased. In traditional Judaism it is a sacred obligation for sons to say the "*Kaddish*" prayer for their deceased parents three times each day during the year after their death, and it is recited by every congregation at every liturgy throughout the year.

"*Kaddish*" may be the most famous Jewish prayer for the dead. It is not, however, the only one. To this day, the beautiful prayer entitled "*El Male Rahamim*" ("O God full of Compassion") is recited during the funeral of every observant Jew:

> O God, full of compassion and exalted in the heights, grant perfect peace in your sheltering presence, among the holy and pure, to the soul of the deceased, who has gone to his eternal home. Master of mercy, we beseech you, remember all the worthy and righteous deeds that he performed in the land of the living. May his soul be bound up in the bond of life. The Lord is his portion. May he rest in peace. And let us say, Amen.[10]

In this prayer we again see the living praying for the salvation of one who has already died and the conviction that such prayers will make a difference; we see, as well, the belief that how one lived one's life on earth will have a profound effect on the way God deals with us in the world to come. This, like the Jewish prayers of the Old Testament, expresses the very heart of the Christian sentiment concerning death and the life after death.

As spiritual heirs of the Jews and as people who were profoundly transformed by belief in the Resurrection of Jesus, the early Christians had an intense belief in judgment and prayers for the dead. Inscriptions on early Christian tombs and the catacombs, especially in Rome, call for prayers to be said for the dead and even spell out the prayers so that the tomb itself would be a never-ending reminder to pray for the deceased person. It is also a fact that all the oldest Eucharistic Prayers extant contain a prayer for the dead, what in Latin is called the *memento mori*, showing that from its very earliest times the Church has brought prayer for the dead into the Mass itself, the very heart of her spiritual life, thus dramatically connecting human death to Jesus's own death and Resurrection and emphasizing once again that the deceased undergo some sort of purification after death. In this connection we are made aware that the most significant prayer we can offer for the deceased is and always will be the Mass itself.

As the Church separated herself from her Jewish parent and grew in both the East and West, different customs and styles developed. Similar thoughts were expressed in sometimes very different language. The Western Church faced a series of heresies over several centuries and then the Protestant Reformation. All this led her to refine her teachings more and more, to be explicit about the details of the faith, to define things clearly and with great precision. The Eastern Church, however, led a different life. After her first few centuries, she was rarely confronted by heretical versions of herself but by a radically different faith: that of Islam. For Eastern Orthodoxy the details did not have to be continually explicated; instead the very essentials of the faith needed to be upheld and defended in the face of a powerful and aggressive religion that was antagonistic to the very essence of Christianity.

Thus, while judgment was never questioned in the Eastern Church, and prayers for the dead were regularly offered, Purgatory remained (and continues to remain) undefined. Although the word might be rarely used, the concept continues to be deeply embedded in Orthodox thought and spirituality as the following beautiful prayer for the dead taken from the Orthodox liturgy clearly shows:

> By Thy resurrection from the dead, O Christ, death no longer hath dominion over those who die in holiness. So, we beseech Thee, give rest to Thy servants in Thy sanctuary and in Abraham's bosom. Grant it to those, who from Adam until now have adored Thee with purity, to our fathers and brothers, to our kinsmen and friends, to all men who have lived by faith and passed on their road to Thee, by a thousand ways, and in all conditions, and make them worthy of the heavenly kingdom.[11]

Here we find the Eastern Church praying fervently not only for its own beloved dead but also for "all men who have lived by faith" and asking God to grant rest to those who may have died centuries before.

The "Hymns of Farewell," which are chanted during the Orthodox (and Byzantine Rite Catholic) funeral liturgy include these words written as if they are said by the soul to those who mourn as it departs earthly life:

> I go to the Lord God my Judge to stand before His judg-
> ment seat and to answer for my deeds. I implore you, pray
> for me that the Savior may be merciful to me on judgment
> day. Behold, we part! Indeed, all human endeavor is vanity.[12]

As we can clearly see, the Eastern awareness of judgment is profound, as is belief in the efficacy of prayers for the dead and an interim state between this earthly life and the joys of eternal life.

With the sole exception of John Wesley, the founder of Methodism, the leading Protestant reformers strenuously denied an interim place of purification for the dead (Purgatory) and thus the usefulness of prayers for the deceased. They never thought, however, of denying a Final Judgment for the individual. In fact they dwelled on it often. This judgment, as it is expressed in the rather somber theologies of Luther and Calvin, can at times seem terrifying, with God's justice and wrath very apparent, and His love and mercy less prominent. Jonathan Edwards, among the best known of American Calvinists of the eighteenth century and a Congregationalist minister, had this to say in 1741 about God's judgment of the human soul:

> The God that holds you over the pit of hell, much as
> one holds a spider, or some loathsome insect, over the fire,
> abhors you and is dreadfully provoked; His wrath towards
> you burns like fire; He looks upon you as being worthy of
> nothing but to be cast into the fire; He is of purer eyes than
> to bear to have you in his sight; you are ten thousand times
> so abominable in His eyes, as the most hateful and venom-
> ous serpent is in ours.[13]

These words seem incredible to the Catholic mind, for while we would never deny the wrath of God, we always acknowledge that His wrath is not only balanced by His love and mercy but is actually a mysterious part of His love and mercy. We also believe that God will never abhor us, even though He certainly will abhor some of our acts. In Edwards's words, God's wrath seems to have totally eclipsed all love, all mercy. It must be noted that most Protestants today would find Edwards's ideas nearly as difficult and foreign as Catholics do, but in the first few centuries of Protestantism this sort of understanding of judgment was common. In it, the encounter of the human soul with the God who is its judge is an experience not merely of awe, fear, and guilt, but of absolute terror.

Wesley, however, whose thought at times can seem very Catholic, believed not only in a somewhat gentler understanding of judgment but also in an intermediate state after earthly life and before the Final Judgment. He also admitted the possibility of "continuing to grow in holiness there," an idea that not unexpectedly scandalized some of his Protestant contemporaries. Once when reprimanded by his (Anglican) bishop for praying for the dead, Wesley replied:

> Your . . . argument is that in a collection of prayers, I cite the words of an ancient liturgy 'for the faithful departed.' Sir, whenever I use those words in the Burial Service, I pray to the same effect, 'that we with all those who are departed in Thy faith and fear, may have our perfect consummation and bliss, both in body and soul,' yea, and whenever I say, 'Thy Kingdom come' — for I mean both the Kingdom of grace and glory.[14]

Wesley's views, however, remained that of a very small minority among Protestants. Julia Ward Howe dramatically articulated the traditional Protestant position that we all face an uncompromising judge after death in "The Battle Hymn of the Republic." Here she famously wrote: "He is sifting out the hearts of men before his judgment seat." We certainly do not see the extremity of Jonathan Edwards here; yet Howe, writing exactly 120 years after Edwards, makes no mention of God's mercy and certainly manages to convey that our judge will be a powerful and harsh one.

Unfortunately, with all its superficiality and skepticism, our present age treats the judgment of God as it does so many things of spiritual importance: it simply ignores it without taking the trouble even to attempt to deny it. Despite the fact that even in this shallow and unthinking time 85 percent of Americans are estimated by serious polls to expect to render some account of their lives to their Maker when they die, the postmodern world remains silent about such things, and we are left with the idea that the most important spiritual realities such as grace and the judgment of God do not exist. God, as He is popularly understood, does not seem much interested in these things.

Nothing could be further from the truth as it is revealed to us in sacred Scripture. For instance, the fact that the Divine Being expects obedience and good behavior from us is vividly preached from the opening chapters of the Book of Genesis to the very last lines of the Apocalypse. There is not a statement of Christ that even suggests that there is no judgment. Quite the contrary: Even though He clearly proclaims the mercy of God to sinners in such parables as that of the Prodigal Son (Luke 15:11-32) and the lost sheep (Luke 15: 3-7), He firmly reminds us of judgment at other times. The incredible pity of Christ for abused and misled souls must always be understood as balanced by His description of the Last Judgment found in the twenty-fifth chapter of the Gospel of Saint Matthew. Here He welcomes the kind and the generous into eternal life, while those who were unresponsive to the needs of others are sent to the "everlasting fires prepared for the devil and his angels."

What Is the Judgment Like? What Is Purgatory Like?

First, we must distinguish between the judgment of the individual at the moment of death, often called the Particular Judgment, and the judgment of all who have ever lived at the end of the ages, called the General Judgment. The particular or immediate judgment of the individual at the hour of death has been proclaimed by ecumenical councils and many authoritative papal teachings from the thirteenth to the fifteenth centuries, when there was a great interest in life after death.[15] There are very convincing sources for such teachings from the Gospels. "Today you will be with me in Paradise" (Luke 23:43), says our Lord to the thief on the cross. "One thing you still lack. Sell all that you have and distribute to the poor, and you will have treasure in heaven; and come, follow me" (Luke 18:22), He tells the rich young man. These and other texts, especially including the parable of Lazarus and the miserly rich man (Luke 16:19-31), all indicate not only that the individual is judged but that this judgment follows the end of our earthly life. It seems to be common sense that if the personhood of the individual — what we call the soul — continues to exist after death, that the final assignment of this person should occur at death, since from that point onward there is no longer any opportunity for either sinful or virtuous free acts, for either merit or blame. Eternity has begun.

There are many depictions of the Particular Judgment. I think the ones that are most interesting are those that are most consistent with the Christian understanding of God, especially from the Gospels. One of these interpretations is given by Saint Catherine of Genoa (1447-1510). A figure very much like Mother Teresa, she was a lay mystic who wrote about her revelations concerning life after death in a most beautiful and dramatic way.[16] We will have reason to refer to these remarkable writings on spiritual dialogue and Purgatory several times, as they have made significant contributions to Catholic teaching on these subjects. Saint Catherine's teachings are often quoted out of context and are even frequently misquoted. We will, however, attempt to be absolutely truthful to her writings and to her profound spiritual insights.

Saint Augustine also wrote extensively about Purgatory and of the purifying or purging fires that are the soul's state after death and before entrance into eternal life and bliss. Augustine was certainly aware that these were not natural fires, because the soul is without any material substance. Many others who were influenced by his writings, however, were not as sophisticated in their thinking, and a great deal of speculation as to the fires of Purgatory began, actually increasing as the centuries passed. While this may seem strange to us today, if we consider the culture in which it took place, we would realize that it is not. During the Dark Ages and the Middle Ages, there was a great effort to get the descendants of the barbarians to behave in a civilized manner. As a result, concepts such as chivalry and personal nobility of character were developed. The noble ideas of many people, especially many saints, filled literature and popular culture. They came to a kind of apex with Saint Francis of Assisi. He was neither a nobleman nor a priest (he was, however, a deacon), but he epitomized the Christian virtues. The other side of this noble preaching of the virtues was to describe in high relief (and great regularity) the punishment of sinners. We must bear in mind the fact that for many people of the time, the distinction between the spiritual and the physical was ambiguous. Heaven really was for them a place beyond the sky; Hell and Purgatory were physical locations, as well. If this is so, it is only logical that the punishing flames of Purgatory would be seen as physical fire rather than spiritual fire.

The classic hymn formerly used in the Requiem Mass and made famous throughout the world by such composers as Mozart, the *"Dies Irae,"* expresses perfectly the attitude toward death and retribution of this time. It describes in high drama not only the punishment of the wicked in Hell but also the temporary punishment that may be remitted after death. It ends with this line: *"Pie Jesu Domine, dona eis requiem"* (Merciful Lord Jesus, give them rest). This hymn by Fra Thomas of Celano, Saint Francis's biographer, or possibly by another Franciscan who remains anonymous, was actually composed for the last Sunday of the Church year, when the liturgy reminds us of the end of the world and the Last Judgment. It later became a standard part of the funeral Mass. I remember quaking with more than a little fear as an altar boy when it was sung at funerals, especially at the phase *"tuba mirum spargens sonnum, per sepulcra regionem coget omnes ante thronum"* ("the awesome trumpet spreads its sound, through the place of tombs calling all before the throne").

In the minds of most Catholics, Purgatory — the interim state after death and before the soul is admitted to the joy of Heaven — was associated with Hell itself, the one difference being that the first was temporary and the other eternal. The reaction to this, of course, was to try to avoid Purgatory altogether through the use of plenary indulgences or though the arrangement of Masses to be offered for oneself after death. This apparently innocent procedure led to many scandalous excesses, which in turn eventually led to the Protestant Reformation and the total denial among most Protestants of an intervening period during which those not entirely prepared to meet the Lord would expiate their sins and be purified.

Unfortunately, Dante, the great Italian poet, entered into this drama and produced a lurid but eloquent description of Purgatory as a temporary Hell. This representation was still popularly held when I was young. At that time, one could even visit churches with mosaic flames around the edges of the dome, which included pictures of Our Lady and the saints pulling naked holy souls out of what looked to be a sea of burning oil. All of this was carried on in the face of a decree of the Council of Trent forbidding people from comparing Purgatory to Hell and presenting it to others as a temporary Hell. We will discuss the different possible outcomes of the Particular Judgment later, but we should try to have a truly Christian idea of the judgment itself.

Purgatory, it must be said, continues to be something with which most Protestants are uneasy, and it places stumbling blocks in the path of many ecumenical discussions. It remains a sad source of division among Christians, but this should not be. One of the most persistent and popular objections to the idea of Purgatory among Protestants, especially Evangelicals, is that it seems in their eyes to diminish the importance of Christ's sacrifice. Even Catholics may wonder about this at times. If, they say, Christ died for the forgiveness of all, how can there still be a need for further cleansing or reparation? The Church, of course, in no way denies that Christ's death on the cross was all sufficient for our salvation and forgiveness. In fact, we see the existence of Purgatory as one aspect or fruit of that great act: the final cleansing offered to us by the divine love that frees us of the last remnants of our sins and makes us worthy of the presence of God.

It is my belief that the denial of Purgatory among Protestants finds its roots in the radical theological ideas of Luther and especially Calvin. These men envisioned God as not only absolute but also so transcendent as to be arbitrary. In Calvin's theology one finds a God who predestines people from before the beginning of time either to Hell or to Heaven. Nothing about a person's life can have any effect on his final outcome; it is simply the arbitrary and inscrutable will of God that determines the fate of every human being. This is the God of Jonathan Edwards, whom we read about earlier in this chapter. This extreme concept of predestination makes the judgment of God incomprehensible, for of what use is judgment if the facts of a person's life have no bearing on how he will be judged and if the judgment has already been in effect since before the world began?

While the Catholic Church firmly maintains that Christ alone pays the price for forgiveness for everyone, including even His Immaculate Mother, the Church also maintains that each person has responsibility for his or her own actions and points to the Gospels to support this. We have only to think again of the parable of Lazarus and the rich man to see the relationship between action and the judgment one receives from God.

The God of Calvin and of Luther is so transcendent that he could arbitrarily decide that theft is good and honesty bad. The rules of the universe, the natural law, mean nothing to such a God, who might simply change them by royal fiat. Beliefs such as absolute predestination were virtually unknown before the Protestant Reformation, and they contradict the concept of God that has been part of the tradition of the Catholic and Orthodox Churches since the very beginning. It is our understanding that God is not arbitrary; that God is a God of true justice, but equally a God of love and mercy. In the Protestantism that was taught by Luther and Calvin, Christ, by His infinite goodness, pays completely for the grace of salvation out of mercy — but a mercy that remains arbitrary. In such a view Purgatory obviously makes no sense. It is the Catholic point of view that arbitrary salvation without personal responsibility or the God-given possibility of shedding our sins in Purgatory make no sense.

Today much of Protestantism has moved far from the ideas of Calvin, Luther, and most of the other reformers, mitigating and even rejecting their doctrines. This change, however, has rarely caused Protestant thinkers to reconsider the possibility of Purgatory, which remains foreign to the Protestant tradition.

Newman's Vision of Purgatory

There are many possible theological opinions we could explore concerning Purgatory, but this is uncalled for in a practical book such as this. The best description I can think of and the one that the interested reader might find most helpful is presented in the epic poem of Cardinal John Henry Newman (1801-1890) called "The Dream of Gerontius."[17] This poem was published twenty years after Newman left the Anglican Church, becoming a Catholic and a priest of the Oratory. After his conversion, this prominent clergyman from Oxford almost completely disappeared from public view for nearly twenty years. With the publication of his *Apologia pro Vita Sua*[18] in 1864, however, Newman began to attract much attention. The appearance of "The Dream of Gerontius" the following year in serial form in a popular weekly periodical attracted even more. It became an immediate and startling success. Everyone appeared to have read it.

"The Dream of Gerontius" is apparently very deeply influenced by the writings of Saint Catherine of Genoa, in which judgment takes place the instant the individual steps into the presence of the Risen Christ. In Newman's poem, Gerontius, a devout old man, dies. He breathes his last surrounded by his family and a priest who are all praying around his bedside. But even after death Gerontius finds himself to be strangely aware. He actually feels better than when he was alive. He says to himself:

> I went to sleep; and now I am refreshed.
> A strange refreshment: for I feel in me
> An inexpressive lightness, and a sense
> Of freedom, as I were at length myself
> And ne'er had been before. How still it is!
> I hear no more the busy beat of time,
> No, nor my fluttering breath, nor struggling pulse;
> Nor does one moment differ from the next.[19]

Here the reader understands Gerontius to be beyond death and time, in a state beyond the illnesses and frailty that plagued him during his earthly life. These have evaporated, to be replaced by lightness and refreshment.

Gerontius is then met by his guardian angel, whose task it is to take him to his judgment. The angel seems to rejoice, saying: "My work is done, my task is o'er, and so I come, taking [the soul of Gerontius] home, for the crown is won, Alleluia, for evermore."[20]

Together the two pass a gaggle of mocking and frightening evil spirits. Gerontius asks his angel why he is not frightened to meet his Judge, as he has feared the judgment of God his whole life long. His angelic partner replies that such an absence of fear is a good sign, noting that Gerontius did not have to be afraid now because he had feared God during his time on earth and lived a good and holy life. Newman describes the ascent into the presence of Christ in the form of a dialogue between the soul of Gerontius and the angel:

SOUL
I go before my Judge.

ANGEL
... Praise to His name!
The eager spirit has darted from my hold,
And, with the intemperate energy of love,
Flies to the dear feet of Emmanuel;
But, ere it reach them, the keen sanctity,
Which with its effluence, like a glory, clothes
And circles round the Crucified, has seized,
And scorched, and shrivelled it; and now it lies
Passive and still before the awful Throne.
O happy, suffering soul! for it is safe,
Consumed, yet quickened by the glance of God.[21]

Here we find the soul of Gerontius approaching "the Crucified," Christ, the God who will be his judge. As the soul draws near, he is so overcome with love for the divine presence that he pulls free of the grasp of the angel and rushes forward toward the throne of Christ. However, still unpurified of his earthly sins, Gerontius, good as he was, cannot bear the presence of the Lord and collapses. He lies inert, as if scorched by the intensity of the divine love. Gerontius suffers terribly, yet he is safe and actually experiences joy, the joy of being near the presence of God:

SOUL
Take me away, and in the lowest deep
There let me be,
And there in hope the lone night-watches keep,
Told out for me.
There, motionless and happy in my pain,
Lone, not forlorn, —
There will I sing my sad perpetual strain,
Until the morn
There will I sing and soothe my stricken breast,
Which ne'er can cease.
To throb, and pine, and languish, till possest
Of its Sole Peace.
There will I sing my absent Lord and Love: –
Take me away,
That sooner I may rise, and go above
And see Him in the truth of everlasting day.[22]

In his brief but terrible encounter with the divine presence, Gerontius sees for the first time his many sins for what they are. He sees how they have damaged him and made him unfit for the joys of Heaven, for the presence of God. He thinks himself worthy of no more than to be taken to "the lowest deep" and left there forever, yearning for the God that he deeply offended and for an instant experienced. Instead of being abandoned, as he believes he should be, however, Gerontius is treated with great gentleness and compassion. Now the angel describes bringing the soul of Gerontius into Purgatory in a most consoling way:

ANGEL
Softy and gently, dearest, sweetest soul,
In my most loving arms I now enfold thee,

And o'er the penal waters, as they roll,
I poise thee, and I lower thee, and hold thee.

And carefully I dip thee in the lake.
And though, without a sob or a resistance,
Dost through the flood thy rapid passage take,
Sinking deep, deeper, into the dim distance.

Angels, to whom the willing task is given,
Shall tend and nurse, and lull thee, as thou liest;
And Masses on the earth, and prayers in heaven
Shall aid thee at the Throne of the Most Highest.

Farewell, but not for ever! Brother dear,
Be brave and patient on thy bed of sorrow;
Swiftly shall pass thy night of trial here.
And I will come and wake thee on the morrow.[23]

His angel has gathered Gerontius up and placed him in Purgatory, which in Newman's understanding is not a place of fire or torment but a place of healing and refreshing waters, a place of gentle cleansing. There, angels assigned to this task will bathe him in the waters of Purgatory and care tenderly for him until he has been healed and properly prepared to enter into the heavenly world. Newman tells us this healing will be aided by "Masses on the earth, and prayers in heaven," and we realize that Gerontius is not alone in his Purgatory — his exile — but is still united with the Mystical Body of Christ, which works constantly to prepare him for the divine presence, to bring him to God.

There is much more to this great poem that we will not be able to examine, but in the few lines we have seen we come to understand Newman's concept of Purgatory. It is very different from the one most of us grew up with. For Newman, Purgatory is a work of the divine mercy, a place of solace and cleansing rather than of torture or punishment. Newman's poem is, of course, highly symbolic; yet the ideas behind it are plausible and consistent with the Scriptures that Newman knew so well and with his own strong faith.

Judgment and Its Results

What shall we say about the glorious encounter with the Son of God experienced by the saints as well as totally innocent infants and small children after earthly death? It is generally taught that Purgatory is not part of their experience; that they go immediately into Heaven — everlasting life. Saint Paul assures us that the complete meaning of this reality has not entered into our minds and hearts, yet Christ describes it as His coming to get us and bringing us into His Father's house. He uses words like, "Come, O blessed of my Father, inherit the kingdom prepared for you from the foundation of the world" (Matthew 25:34). These are very beautiful and divinely reassuring words, but their full and glorious meaning still remains impossible for our limited minds and understanding to grasp.

As we cannot fully grasp the eternal joy of Heaven, we can hardly imagine the absolute horror that must seize a person leaving this world who learns he is lost forever. We will have relatively little to say about this because, as I noted previously, I can't believe that those who read this book are in real danger of that horrible outcome. As we consider these possibilities, we should begin by realizing that the judgment of the living God is an essential consequence of our human dignity as free beings. Because we are creatures endowed with freedom — a freedom that bestows great dignity on us — we can only achieve our real worth by being held accountable for what we do. This is why people with religious convictions — regardless of their theology and no matter what faith they belong to — still expect some kind of judgment.

While most world religions teach us that we have some kind of life after death and that the quality of that life is determined by one's judgment, Christianity alone promises eternal life, not merely in the realm of the Sovereign of the universe, but in our Father's house. This is why Christians need to take our Final Judgment so seriously and with much dependence on the mercy of God and the grace of Christ. No one has so great a hope as a Christian. Consequently, no one should take judgment more seriously.

Chapter Three

ETERNAL PUNISHMENT

---

*"Save us from final damnation,
and count us among those you have chosen."*

EUCHARISTIC PRAYER I

No one can deny the possibility of the eternal loss of the vision of God promised to the saved, although many attempts have been made — sometimes by kindly and noble souls — to question this possibility. During the early years of the Church, Origen of Alexandria, one of the Church Fathers, held to the belief that after a time of cleansing every soul would eventually be admitted into the presence of God. Origen was among the greatest of the early Church's theologians, but on this point he erred greatly. It is significant that he, almost alone among the Fathers, has not been canonized. It is not unreasonable to say that his inability to accept Jesus' plain words on the possibility of eternal loss is among the explanations for this.

The hope of universal salvation is obviously an attractive one — a tempting one — and it has recurred over and over again throughout the centuries. In fact, there was even a Protestant body that claimed this as their distinguishing principle. Called the Universalist Church and founded in 1866, this body taught that ultimately all souls would be reconciled with God. Rejected by most Protestants, this church was never large, and in less than a century was absorbed into Unitarianism. In our own time, several theological writers, including Hans Urs von Balthasar, the distinguished Swiss theologian, have once again raised the question: "Dare we hope that no one is lost forever?" The origin of this question is not based on divine revelation from the Bible, which alone can give an authoritative answer. It springs, rather, from the compassion of the human heart as well as a false kind of humanism, which permeates much of our modern thinking. The simple fact is that Christ's words in the Gospel give the highest possible authority to the belief in eternal punishment. The words of several New Testament writers — especially those of Saint Paul and the author of the Apocalypse — when considered with Christ's teachings, make the existence of Hell undeniable. And we must never forget that the perfection of God's justice demands it.

Think about the appalling wickedness that one encounters in human history. Political movements that are guilty of large-scale atrocities and nearly unimaginable cruelties are not unusual. The Holocaust is the best-known example of this, but it is far from the only one. There have been numerous other horrors perpetrated by the tyrants who were so common during the twentieth century.

Unspeakable acts of brutality can be committed on a far smaller scale, as well. Individual acts of cruelty and crime that deprive the innocent of life and the possibility of happiness occur often in our world, and this has always been the case. Our Lord points out this special evil, and He uses words of great seriousness in doing so. When speaking, for example, about the scandalizing of the young, He clearly states that for someone responsible for such evil it would be better "if a millstone were hung round his neck and he were cast into the sea" (Luke 17:2). Christ makes it plain that the consequences of the betrayal of innocence are dire. In a crime as horrible as Judas' betrayal of the innocent Word Incarnate, Christ said that it would be better if Judas had never been born (Matthew 26:24). These words, of course, inevitably bring a contemporary betrayal of innocence to mind, that of the abuse of the young by some clergy. Is it really unreasonable to believe that those who commit such sins willingly, repeatedly, and wholeheartedly and remain unrepentant should merit eternal punishment? Pope John Paul II, when discussing these tragic and sinful activities, used the term "*mysterium iniquitatis,*" the mystery of iniquity, and this is what we are faced with in such instances — the mystery of an evil that springs up in the human heart and takes over a person's life.

Hellish human enterprises such as the slavery that existed in this country before the Civil War, and abortion, which has become so common and accepted in our own time, are instances of profound sin that were politically sanctioned and culturally accepted. These are also reasons for those involved to fear the eternal justice of the Creator. Entire societies seem to lose the ability to distinguish right from wrong, to see the worth inherent in every human being. Again we are faced with the "*mysterium iniquitatis.*" Again we wonder how the sinfulness of such acts can be denied. The longer we contemplate human iniquity, the more we are inclined to believe it must have profound consequences, that the existence of Hell is irrefutable. But who among us really goes to Hell?

Who Goes to Hell?

Many questions come into focus once we admit the reality of Hell. The first of these is: How common is this terrible fate? In a remarkable article with the engaging title "The Population of Hell," the late Cardinal Avery Dulles examined the history of attitudes toward eternal damnation throughout Church history. At times it seemed that — in the popular estimation, at least — there were many lost souls. At other times, such as our own, the possibility or at least the likelihood of damnation has been rather blithely dismissed by far too many. Pope Benedict XVI, however, clearly believes that Hell is a possibility for us all. In *Spe Salvi* he writes:

> There can be people who have totally destroyed their desire for truth and readiness to love, people for whom everything has become a lie, people who have lived for hatred and have suppressed all love within themselves. This is a terrifying thought, but alarming profiles of this type can be seen in certain figures of our own history. In such people all would be beyond remedy and the destruction of good would be irrevocable: this is what we mean by the word Hell.[24]

Although it is unlikely that the serious Christian who tries to live a life of faithful discipleship will find himself in the position of facing the eternal loss of Hell, it remains always a possibility for each one of us. And we must remember that this awful possibility is one that is not imposed on us by God, but one we impose upon ourselves. In the words of Pope John Paul II:

> "Eternal damnation" ... is not attributed to God's initiative because in his merciful love he can only desire the salvation of the beings he created. In reality, it is the creature who closes himself to his love. Damnation consists precisely in definitive separation from God, freely chosen by the human person and confirmed with death that seals his choice for ever. God's judgment ratifies this state.[25]

It is vital, therefore, to take the meanings of Christ's words "to watch and pray," to "seek first his kingdom and his righteousness" (Matthew 6:33) and "enter by the narrow gate" (Matthew 7:13) seriously. Saint Paul tells us that even though our deformed conscience may not trouble us, we are not justified thereby.[26] We must never forget that although we can trust completely in the love of our heavenly Father, we must do our part every day of our lives. The forces of the *"mysterium iniquitatis"* are strong and all-pervasive as they work to pull us away from God. We must be aware of the possibility of eternal loss constantly. We must be vigilant that we remain in a state of grace, for if that is not the case at the moment of our death, hope of eternal salvation is lost — lost by us and for us. To be in the state of grace means that Christ lives within us. If we extinguish the life of Christ in us through serious sin, if we banish Him from our souls, we have separated ourselves and alienated ourselves from God. We have chosen eternal nothingness. We have chosen Hell.

For any serious reader of this book, it might be literally foolish and lacking in trust in God to focus unduly on the fear of Hell, but we must at the same time keep the possibility in mind that we could all slip and fall a very great distance without the help of God's grace. At the same time, we need to be concerned about those who can be led astray or who already appear to be turning away from God and the Kingdom promised by Christ. It is necessary to pray for those in danger of eternal loss as well as to reach out to them.

These are actions very motivated by the scriptural pronouncements, especially those of Christ about the dreadful possibility of eternal loss. They are motivated, as well, by Christian charity, a virtue that can be ours through the workings of the Holy Spirit.

In speaking or thinking about the possibility of eternal damnation in all its awesome terror and sadness, it is appropriate also to speak of the evil spirits, the dark angels who, according to Scripture, have intruded repeatedly into salvation history and rather obviously into the history of the world. In fact, it is such a spirit whom the writers of Genesis tell us engineered the Fall of Man. The Serpent in the Garden of Eden has always been identified as Satan — a word that in Hebrew means "adversary." This dark spirit is indeed the adversary of man, the one who has caused us to rupture our relationship with God, the one who allowed death to enter our lives, the one who yearns for us to join him in the eternal emptiness of an existence devoid of the Divine Presence. In much of popular literature and art Satan is shown as existing in ferocious and endless fire; and, as we have seen elsewhere, fire has often been the primary image of the suffering experienced by the soul that is denied the presence of God.

There has been throughout history, however, another way of envisioning the pains of Hell beside that of a consuming fire — ice. In Dante's *Inferno*, Satan stands in the very depths of Hell, immobile and imprisoned in a huge block of ice. The greatest sinners of history surround him, also frozen and encased. There is no warmth in their lives — no warmth of love. Cold has no independent existence: It is simply the absence of warmth. The less warmth there is, the colder things become. In Dante's vision of Hell, every shred of warmth has been drained away. Satan and those who have sinned greatly, their skin turned blue, exist in the imprisoning nothingness of absolute cold, in the emptiness that is revealed when all love is obliterated. This is the agony of Hell, the total lack of contact with the love of God, the presence of God. Dante is an artist and not a theologian, so we must not mistake his great poem for a theological treatise, but he has captured something about the essence of Hell — of eternity without God — that is both terrifying and profound.

Anyone who remembers the Second World War, anyone who recalls the horrors of Stalinist Russia, the killing fields of southeast Asia, the savage brutality of Rwanda and Uganda and so many other human tragedies, anyone who has heard of an individual of renowned goodness suddenly performing a horrible and inexplicable act of cruelty, should have at least a suspicion that the "*mysterium iniquitatis*" might not always be the result of human failure alone. At times, human atrocities seem so extreme and yet so commonplace that one senses we may not be capable of all this horror on our own, that in the extremity of our sinfulness we might be misled by some other forces. I believe this is sometimes true, and I believe that these forces are what Scripture identifies as Satan and his minions.

It would be unwise in times like ours to lose sight of this grim reality. Way back in the 1970s Pope Paul VI warned us that we should be aware of the influence of satanic forces in human society; in fact, he said "from some fissure the smoke of Satan has entered the temple of God,"[27] meaning that evil forces were even to be found within the Church itself.

Pope Leo XIII, a very urbane and sophisticated man who died in 1903, understood such things well and composed a beautiful prayer to Saint Michael. Many of us remember the popular form of it that was always recited at the end of Mass up to the 1960s:

Saint Michael the Archangel,
defend us in battle.
Be our protection against the wickedness and snares of
the devil.
May God rebuke him, we humbly pray;
and do thou, O Prince of the Heavenly Host —
by the Divine Power of God —
cast into hell, Satan and all the evil spirits,
who roam throughout the world seeking the ruin of
souls.

One should read that prayer carefully and meditate on its meaning because chances are that every one of my readers has at times encountered the influence of the fallen and dark angels, "who roam throughout the world seeking the ruin of souls."

All of this is cause for concern, of course. The power of evil is real, but we must never forget that God's power is far greater; in fact, it is absolute. In turning to Him wholeheartedly in prayer and in deed, we can vanquish any evil force. We must never forget that "with God all things are possible." In the writings of Saint Faustina, through whom God has given us the beautiful devotion to the Divine Mercy, we read that Christ comes to the soul three times at the moment of death; three times Christ offers salvation. It is up to us to turn from our sins and transgressions and humbly accept what God so graciously offers us.

The possibility of eternal loss is with us always, but there is no reason to come to this tragic fate. We must turn to Christ, for in Him we can be saved from "the loss of Heaven and the pains of Hell."

Chapter Four

THE EXPERIENCE OF PURGATION

The Interim State Before Eternal Life

*"There is no joy save that in paradise to be compared
to the joy of the souls in purgatory."*

SAINT CATHERINE OF GENOA

Anyone growing up in the Catholic world before Vatican II was very well aware of Purgatory and was familiar with praying for the holy souls who were there. The history of the belief in an interim state between this life and eternal life is fascinating, as we have seen in Chapter Two. We have also seen that Purgatory has been envisioned in a great many different ways, ranging from a terrible suburb of Hell to a healing bath in which the soul is cared for by the angels of Purgatory, as in "The Dream of Gerontius."

Following up on the Hebrew idea of an interim state after death and before Heaven, Christians of the very early Church found it quite natural to pray that the deceased would be relieved of the effects of their sins. From those very early days, the existence of a state of purgation after death has been a part of the fabric of the Church's teachings; it was never seriously questioned anywhere or at any time throughout the Christian world until the Protestant Reformation began in the sixteenth century, at which time and for a variety of tragic reasons it was rejected by the reformers.

To understand the doctrine of Purgatory, it is necessary to be aware of the effects of sins. Mortal sin or deadly sin utterly destroys a person's relationship with God, the source of life. This relationship is called grace, and a person who is in this relationship is said to be in the state of grace. Grace is won for us by Christ alone, and without it there can be no possibility of eternal life. This is because eternal life belongs only to God, the Holy Trinity, and the participation of human beings in eternal life is a pure gift: for that reason it is called grace. This even extends to the Mother of God, the Blessed Virgin Mary, who is called "Our Lady of Grace" and whom the angel greets at the Annunciation as "full of grace."

Of course, most offenses against God are not so serious. Each of us spends almost every day of our lives committing one small sin after another. These we call venial sins, offenses that injure our relationship with our heavenly Father but do not destroy it, that partially separate us from God rather than completely rupture our relationship with Him. Venial sins fall into two distinct categories. The first consists of sins committed with distraction or out of human weakness. Here we also include even serious sins committed because of ignorance, fear, or compulsion, and the sins we commit almost against our will out of concupiscence.

The second category is of much greater seriousness. Here we find the completely deliberate sins concerning small matters such as lying, gossiping, the sins that betray a lack of charity to others, the many sad sins of needless unkindness. This kind of sin in small or venial matters seems trivial to many, but it is not. It is morally the second worst reality in existence because it is done deliberately as an offense against God. A seriously wrong act done out of weakness or inadvertence or with a divided will is less of an offense than the small very deliberate act done knowingly against the will of God. While such deeds may not cause the loss of the state of grace, they are large steps away from growth in the spiritual life and preclude any kind of progress in the journey toward God unless they are effectively repented of.

Sin has two effects on the individual in addition to dishonoring God. The first effect is the alienation from God of which we have spoken. The second is what we call temporal punishment. Here we must be careful to understand that temporal punishment is distinct from the eternal punishment of Hell. Temporal punishment is a necessary result of an offense against the justice and holiness of God. God is unblemished holiness, justice, and love, and He calls us to walk in His ways. When we fail — especially when we fail deliberately — and do things to others that may be harmful and completely unjust, we offend God's justice and reject His love. We may, and often do, ask for forgiveness, and so when we die we are in the state of grace. But in our sinning we have done harm that we lack the power to undo. We have incurred a debt that must be paid in some way. We have changed. We have become less than we were, less than God meant us to be. As Pope Benedict XVI says: "Evildoers, in the end, do not sit at table at the eternal banquet beside their victims without distinction, as though nothing had happened."[28] There needs to be some kind of fulfillment of God's justice, even for the repentant. This is what temporal punishment means. Sometimes the debt is paid in this life; often it is not, and this is the reason — the need — for Purgatory.

Purgatory: A Gift of Love

Purgatory — the idea of a passage from this life into eternal life — is an extraordinary gift of God, one that vividly demonstrates our heavenly Father's extravagant love for us. It is indeed unfortunate that many Catholics today have very little understanding of the depth and astonishing beauty inherent in the doctrine of Purgatory, little comprehension of what it says of the relationship that God offers us. Often they even seem to want to reject it, saying (as do most Protestants) that "since Christ's death on the cross has paid our debt to God for sin," there is no need for any such doctrine as that of Purgatory. This is a sad misunderstanding and a great misreading of sacred Scripture. It is also an enormous underestimation of God's love for us. Of course, Christ's sacrifice was sufficient to save all humankind. How could it be otherwise? But in the doctrine of Purgatory we find revealed the God who not only loves but also respects His human creation, the God who yearns for us to work with Him for our salvation and that of all humankind. In Christ's sacrifice we find perfect — unlimited — salvation offered to us at every instant of our lives, but it is never forced on us. God gives us the incomparable gift of free will and refuses to take it away from us even though this gift enables us to make the constant excursions into sinfulness that characterize every human life. Purgatory doesn't deny that sinfulness; it does not cover it up. It heals it, cleansing the human soul, gently and lovingly making us into the beings God wants us to be.

In the doctrine of Purgatory we find a God who sees His human creatures as perfectible, capable of maturity, who does not simply disregard our sins as an indulgent parent might disregard the wrongdoings of a small child, but allows us to work with Him to free ourselves of them, to transcend them. In bestowing freedom upon us, our heavenly Father has permitted us to sin and to sin greatly. But He has also permitted us to become spiritual adults, to be responsible for "what we have done and what we have failed to do." In the doctrine of Purgatory we see an aspect of this spiritual adulthood; we see that our mature acts have consequences, that all our choices have meaning.

In the doctrine of Purgatory the Church stands firmly with Saint Paul, who wrote: "Now I rejoice in my sufferings for your sake, and in my flesh I complete what is lacking in Christ's afflictions for the sake of his body, that is, the church" (Colossians 1:24). What is "lacking in Christ's afflictions"? Absolutely nothing, and Saint Paul is very aware of this. Yet he is also very aware that God wants the ultimate salvation of all to be (at least in part) the work of all, and so this great saint rejoices in the ability to suffer in this life and in the next, to join his little sufferings to the great sufferings of Jesus, to play his role in God's ongoing work of redemption.

The justification for the doctrine of Purgatory can be found in many biblical quotations, especially in some of the writings of Saint Paul, as we shall soon see. The Church, from the earliest Fathers to the present, has been profoundly influenced by these words and unfailingly upheld the doctrine of Purgatory. Our present Holy Father has addressed this problem beautifully and perceptively in his encyclical entitled *Spe Salvi,* saying:

> For the great majority of people — we may suppose — there remains in the depths of their being an ultimate interior openness to truth, to love, to God. In the concrete choices of life, however, it is covered over by ever new compromises with evil — much filth covers purity, but the thirst for purity

remains and it still constantly re-emerges from all that is base and remains present in the soul. What happens to such individuals when they appear before the Judge? Will all the impurity they have amassed through life suddenly cease to matter?[29]

In these words we see the obvious need for Purgatory; and we can see it not only as a need but also as a gift of love offered to sinful man by God. It is God's way of freeing us from all that is impure, from the residue of our many sins. Christ's death on the cross redeems us, of course, but clearly it does not restore mankind to the state we enjoyed before the mysterious Fall of our first parents. Christ's sacrifice could have brought us back to the Garden of Eden, but it did not, and this is God's choice. Death and sickness, pain and suffering are very obviously still part of our lives: so are our sins, our deliberate turnings away from God. Our lives are pilgrimages; they are meant to be a gradual return to that blessed state that existed in the Garden of Eden, a return brilliantly begun but not ended with Christ's death and Resurrection. We are on a slow, steady journey that commences at our conception and continues even after our bodily death until it finally reaches its conclusion in the awesome presence of God.

When writing of Purgatory, Pope Benedict XVI asks, "Will all the impurity [we] have amassed through life suddenly cease to matter?" We can answer with the Holy Father that it does matter, but through our temporal punishments either in this life or beyond it we are given the great gift of shedding this impurity by uniting our sufferings to those of Christ, of participating in a small way in His great act of redemption. In this we are united to the whole Church, the entire Body of Christ, in finally ridding God's creation of sin and evil, of all that is impure, of playing our very small but absolutely unique part in the redemption of ourselves and others.

The existence of Purgatory is necessitated by God's justice, but we should never think of Purgatory only as a way to pay the debt of sin. That would be a very incomplete understanding of it. Purgatory is, as we have said, also a most profound expression of God's love; for, in the words of the *Catechism of the Catholic Church*:

"All who died in God's grace and friendship, but still imperfectly purified, are indeed assured of their eternal salvation; but after death they undergo purification, so as to achieve the holiness necessary to enter the joy of heaven" (n. 1030). What love we see in these words. What joy must lie beneath the suffering of the souls in Purgatory, for to them salvation is assured and can never be taken away. They know, even as they yearn to be in God's presence, that Purgatory is His way of making a place for them with Him, of making them capable of being in His presence. Purgatory can be thought of as a pathway God has made to bring us to Him as the pure and unstained souls He had meant us to be from the beginning. Purgatory is the unshakable knowledge that we will experience the divine presence.

Purgatory as Revealed in the New Testament and the Writings of the Fathers

As we have seen, Purgatory is strongly hinted at in the Old Testament. There are several New Testament texts, as well, which appear to refer to the kind of cleansing, purifying, and liberating punishment that are characteristic of Purgatory. Perhaps the most obvious is the statement of Jesus that we find in the Gospel of Saint Matthew. Here Jesus warns us: "... if you are offering your gift at the altar, and there remember that your brother has something against you, leave your gift there before the altar and go; first be reconciled to your brother, and then come and offer your gift" (Matthew 5:23-24). Christ then adds: "Make friends quickly with your accuser, while you are going with him to court, lest your accuser hand you over to the judge, and the judge to the guard, and you be put in prison; truly I say to you, you will never get out till you have paid the last penny" (Matthew 5:25-26).

We can easily read this quotation as referring to the heavenly altar, which we all hope to come to at the end of our lives. Jesus is telling us quite clearly that this altar is unapproachable for us as long as we remain in our sins. Some reparation must be made for our many transgressions, the defects of our lives that show themselves most tellingly in our relationships with our brothers and sisters. This reparation can, of course, take place to a certain extent during our earthly lives. Some of it cannot and remains until after, when the cleansing of Purgatory finally makes us able to stand at the eternal altar of God.

The last line of this quotation — "you will never get out till you have paid the last penny" — can easily be overlooked, but it is important. If one cannot be released until the final payment is made, then it is clear that release is possible. Therefore, we are speaking of a place of temporary punishment — what we call Purgatory.

Another text which at first seems not to have anything to do with Purgatory, but if pondered, seems almost an explicit proclamation of it, is Matthew 12:32: "And whoever says a word against the Son of man will be forgiven; but whoever speaks against the Holy Spirit will not be forgiven, either in this age or in the age to come." Does this not imply that some sins can be (and are) forgiven in "the age to come?" If such is true, where would they be forgiven? Certainly, this would not take place in Heaven, as no sin can exist there. It is equally impossible that forgiveness would take place in Hell, for Hell is that state of being that is by definition beyond forgiveness. Therefore, there is something else in the "age to come," a place where forgiveness is possible, a place of purification — Purgatory.

Yet another text that many relate to Purgatory is Saint Paul's comparison of the Christian life to a structure each one of us builds on the foundation of Christ:

> For no other foundation can any one lay than that which is laid, which is Jesus Christ. Now if any one builds on the foundation with gold, silver, precious stones, wood, hay, straw — each man's work will become manifest; for the Day will disclose it, because it will be revealed with fire, and the fire will test what sort of work each one has done. If the work which any man has built on the foundation survives, he will receive a reward. If any man's work is burned up, he will suffer loss, though he himself will be saved, but only as through fire. (1 Corinthians 3:11-15)

Here Saint Paul is reminding us that our every action has eternal value — either for good or bad, for it is eternity alone that gives our actions value and meaning. He compares human life to the building of a house. The house is built upon the foundation of Jesus Christ using six materials: three durable and precious ones, all of striking brilliance, and three of little worth that can easily be consumed by fire. We each use these materials to varying degrees in building the house that is our life. The precious materials represent our actions that are performed in perfect charity; we build with lesser materials when our actions are performed in charity but tainted by venial (not mortal) sinfulness, the undue attachment to the things of this world. Saint Paul reminds us that the house that we build will face a fire at the end of our lives, one that will consume all the lesser material — all that is unworthy — and leave only what is brilliant to endure for eternity. This fire is the fire of Purgatory, which burns away the defects in our character caused by the undue attachments to the things of this world and makes us fit for God's presence in eternal life.

The First Letter of Saint Peter contains some important lines that relate to the state that we have come to call Purgatory:

> Blessed be the God and Father of our Lord Jesus Christ! By his great mercy we have been born anew to a living hope through the resurrection of Jesus Christ from the dead, and to an inheritance which is imperishable, undefiled, and unfading, kept in heaven for you, who by God's power are guarded through faith for a salvation ready to be revealed in the last time. In this you rejoice, though now for a little while you may have to suffer various trials, so that the genuineness of your faith, more precious than gold which though perishable is tested by fire, may redound to praise and glory and honor at the revelation of Jesus Christ. (1 Peter 1: 3-7)

Here Saint Peter speaks of our ultimate destination, which is Heaven. We are to make entrance into this destination through fires that will test and purify us like the gold to which he refers. These "fires" can be understood in two ways: as earthly trials and as trials that will occur after death and before we encounter the presence of God.

Beyond the Bible, explicit statements about an intervening state between earthly death and eternal life begin very early in Christian history. Among the first seem to be those by the ancient Christian writer Tertullian (c. A.D. 160 to c. A.D. 220, the first Father of the Church to write in Latin rather than Greek. He was quickly followed by Saints Cyprian of Carthage (died in 258), Cyril of Jerusalem (c. 315 to c. 386), and Gregory of Nyssa (died c. 385), who wrote: "Just as those who refine gold from the dross which it contains not only get this base alloy to melt in the fire, but are obliged to melt the pure gold along with the alloy, and then while this last is being consumed in the purgatorial fire the soul that is welded to this evil must inevitably be in the fire too, until the spurious material alloy is consumed and annihilated...."[30] Saint Augustine, certainly among the greatest of the early Fathers of the Church, had no doubt about Purgatory. This can be seen often in his voluminous writings, including in this quotation taken from his masterpiece, *The City of God*: "Temporal punishments are suffered by some in this life only, by some after death, by some both here and hereafter, but all of them before the last and strictest judgment."[31] It is a well-known fact that with no apologies or arguments Saint Augustine asked for prayers for his deceased parents and, as we have said, even explicitly writes of the purifying fires of that state before Heaven, thus inadvertently giving Purgatory its name.[32] Augustine's own mother, Saint Monica, on her deathbed showed no interest whatsoever in being buried in her homeland (an unusual thing at the time), but she took great pains to admonish her sons to remember their mother at the altar of God after her death.[33]

Belief in an intermediate state between death and Heaven was not limited to the Church's early theologians but was common among simple people, as well. As we have stated, there is abundant evidence in the ancient tombs of Christians that praying for the dead was a regular practice. Such prayer is incontrovertible evidence in the belief in an interim state. Over the course of the centuries, besides prayer for the dead, we find increasing numbers of references to Purgatory in Christian writings. These are listed extensively in the *Companion to the Catechism of the Catholic Church* and include citations of writings made throughout the two-thousand-year history of the Church.

Among the clearest and most dramatic are statements from Ecumenical Councils. These repeatedly and unambiguously affirmed both the existence of Purgatory and the importance of prayer for the dead. For instance, a decree of the Second Council of Lyons in 1274 states: "... if those truly penitent have departed in the love of God, before they have made satisfaction by worthy fruits of penance for sins of commission and omission, the souls of these are cleansed after death by purgatorial or purifying punishments... and to relieve punishments of this kind, the offerings of the living faithful are of advantage to these, namely the sacrifices of Masses, prayers, alms, and other duties of piety...."[34] The Council of Florence, a little more than a century and a half later, virtually repeated the words of the Fathers of the Council of Lyons, strongly affirming the Church's belief both in Purgatory and the efficacy of prayers for the deceased.

The most comprehensive statement on the belief in Purgatory, however, was given by the Council of Trent in strong reaction to the Protestant repudiation of this doctrine:

> Since the Catholic Church, instructed by the Holy Spirit, in conformity with the sacred writings and the ancient tradition of the Fathers in sacred councils, and very recently in this ecumenical Synod, has taught that there is a purgatory, and that the souls detained there are assisted by the suffrages of the faithful, and especially by the acceptable sacrifice of the altar, the holy Synod commands the bishops that they insist that the sound doctrine of purgatory, which has been transmitted by the holy Fathers and holy Councils, be believed by the faithful of Christ, be maintained, taught, and everywhere preached.[35]

What Is Purgatory Like?

In the past much has been made of the fire of Purgatory. As we mentioned in Chapter Two, Saint Augustine speaks of the purging flames, although he certainly was aware that these did not refer to physical fire. The idea of fire is obviously related to the words of Saint Paul in the quotation from his First Letter to the Corinthians (1 Corinthians 3:11-15), although it may also find some of its roots in the early Jewish concept of *Gehenna*, a purgatorial state that came to be identified with the pit of fire written about by the Prophet Isaiah.[36] A combination of fear, anticipation, and a desire to get others to lead really well-behaved lives led to a whole literature and many popular ideas about the nature of Purgatory as a temporary Hell, although this is obviously a contradiction in terms.

We have mentioned already the great mystic of Purgatory, Saint Catherine of Genoa. Her writings, which are considered private revelations rather than speculative theologizing, are so interesting that a sizable citation of her works needs to be given. Speaking of the holy souls in Purgatory, Saint Catherine writes:

> Such is their joy in God's will, in His pleasure
> that they have no concern for themselves
> but dwell only in their joy in God's ordinance
> in having Him do what He will.
> They see only the goodness of God,
> His mercy toward men....
> Only once do the souls understand
> the reason for their purgatory:
> the moment in which they leave this life.
> After that moment, that knowledge disappears.
> Immersed in charity, incapable of deviating from it,
> they can only will or desire pure love.
> There is no joy save that in paradise
> to be compared to the joy of the souls in purgatory.
> This joy increases day by day
> because of the way in which the love of God
> corresponds to that of the soul,
> Since the impediment to that love is worn away daily.
> This impediment is the rust of sin.
> As it is consumed
> The soul is more and more open to God's love....[37]

She goes on to extol the love of God for His creations, including the sinful souls of man:

All goodness
is a participation in God and His love for His creatures.
God loves irrational creatures
and His love provides for them;
in the case of mankind, however,
His love manifests itself in greater or lesser degree
according to the impediments that block His love.
When a soul is close to its first creation,
pure and unstained,
the instinct for beatitude asserts itself
with such impetus and fiery charity
that any impediment becomes unbearable.
The more the soul is aware of that impediment,
the greater its suffering.
The souls in purgatory have no sin in them,
nor is there any impediment between them and God.
Their only suffering lies in what holds them back.[38]

In Saint Catherine's vision, the soul's eventual entrance into the presence of God after purgation is a moment of searing intensity and overwhelming love, a moment almost of ecstatic union between the soul and its Creator:

... for when God sees the Soul pure as it was in its origins
He tugs at it with a glance,
Draws it and binds it to Himself with a fiery love
that by itself could annihilate the immortal soul.
In so acting, God so transforms the soul in Him
that it knows nothing other than God;
and he continues to draw it up into His fiery love
until He restores it
to that pure state from which it first issued.
As it is being drawn upwards
The soul feels itself melting
In the fire of that love of its sweet God,

For He will not cease
until He has brought the soul to its perfection.
That is why the soul seeks to cast off
Any and all impediments,
So that it can be lifted up to God
And such impediments
are the cause of the suffering of the souls in purgatory.[39]

As we have seen, these revelations appear to have strongly influenced Cardinal Newman in his writing of "The Dream of Gerontius." Although Saint Catherine's description is certainly challenging and serious, it completely lacks the horror of many writings about Purgatory that were composed even into the twentieth century.[40] A very positive view of the interim state between earthly life and Heaven — one in keeping with the ideas of Saint Catherine — is given in *Lumen Gentium*, an important decree of the Second Vatican Council:

When the Lord will come in glory, and all the angels with him (cf. Mt 25:31), death will be no more and all things will be subject to him (cf. 1 Cor 15:26-27). But at the present time some of his disciples are pilgrims on earth. Others have died and are being purified, while still others are in glory, contemplating "in full light, God himself triune and one, exactly as he is." All of us, however, in varying degrees and in different ways share in the same charity towards God and our neighbors, and we all sing the one hymn of glory to our God. All, indeed, all who are of Christ and have his spirit form one Church and in Christ cleave together (Eph 4:16). So it is that the union of the wayfarers with the brethren who sleep in the peace of Christ is in no way interrupted, but on the contrary, according to the constant faith of the Church, this union is reinforced by an exchange of spiritual goods. Being more closely united to Christ, those who dwell in heaven fix the whole Church more firmly in holiness...."[41]

Can We Help the Souls in Purgatory?

That the prayers of the believer said on earth can benefit those in Purgatory is a belief that has been held since the early Church — in fact we have seen that such beliefs precede the existence of the Church and are found in the Old Testament itself. Pope Benedict XVI has taken up this topic in a most interesting way. When he answers the question "How can a third person intervene in the encounter of purification between the Savior and Judge?" he reminds us that no man is an island entirely to himself. He reminds us, as well, that our lives are involved with one another, that we are all intertwined through innumerable interactions. He says:

> No one lives alone. No one sins alone. No one is saved alone. The lives of others continually spill over into mine: in what I think, say, do and achieve. And conversely, my life spills over into that of others: for better and for worse. So my prayer for another is not something extraneous to that person, something external, not even after death. In the interconnectedness of Being, my gratitude to the other — my prayer for him — can play a small part in his purification. And for that there is no need to convert earthly time into God's time: in the communion of souls simple terrestrial time is superseded. It is never too late to touch the heart of another, nor is it ever in vain. [42]

We find in these beautiful words of our present Holy Father a reflection of words written two thousand years ago by the first Bishop of Rome, Saint Peter: "With the Lord one day is as a thousand years, and a thousand years as one day" (2 Peter 3:8).

Our prayers for the dead should not be time bound. As often occurs with elderly people, the vast catalog of memory regularly brings to my mind faces of people from the past, even the far distant past. Oftentimes we think of people who played little or no real part in our lives. Occasionally those who have hurt us or treated us badly will come to mind with no apparent reason and with little relationship to what is going on at the present moment. I have determined to make such memories an opportunity for simple prayer for all — friends and foes alike — on their journey to God. This can be a beautiful and faith-filled use of the experience of growing old.

Can They Pray for Us?

Prayer to the holy souls is a devout custom and one that is part of my life. How can they hear us or be aware of our intercession for them? Here we have only to consider how Our Lady or any saint in Heaven can hear our prayers. They are obviously not here with us on earth. Prayer to the saints makes sense only when we consider the omniscience and omnipresence of God. He is everywhere and knows all things. If we address a saint in Heaven, canonized or uncanonized, then can we not also ask our blessed Lord to make our loved ones on their journey to God aware of our request for their prayers? This is a beautiful and sensible application of the doctrine of the Mystical Body of Christ. The holy souls are not left out of Christ's Mystical Body. In fact, they are much more secure in their membership than we are.

Can We Reduce Our Own Purgatory?

The punishment of Purgatory is twofold: the fulfillment of divine justice, or temporal punishment, and the interior purification of the whole person from sinful inclinations and selfishness. The Church teaches us that prayer and especially the devout participation in Holy Mass, the saving sacrifice of Christ, can reduce temporal punishment, as can a favor of the Church in the form of a well-earned indulgence. The spiritual life — that is, growth in holiness and the overcoming of vices — begins in this life. The practice of virtue and the patient enduring of suffering can certainly free us from selfishness and self-love. One often hears it said of a person who endured a painful death: "He had his Purgatory on earth." This observation dovetails with the words of Saint Catherine of Genoa: "We have begun our Purgatory even now."

The wise words of Samuel Johnson to his biographer, Boswell, are worth recalling as a breath of common sense. When Boswell, a Calvinist, complained to Johnson, who was Anglican but pro-Catholic, that Catholics believed in Purgatory, Johnson replied: "Why, Sir, it is a very harmless doctrine. They are of the opinion that the generality of mankind are neither so obstinately wicked as to deserve everlasting punishment, nor so good as to merit being admitted into the society of blessed spirits; and therefore that God is graciously pleased to allow a middle state, where they may be purified by certain degrees of suffering. You see, Sir, there is nothing unreasonable in this."[43]

Apparently shocked at Johnson's words, Boswell continued with: "But then, Sir, their Masses for the dead?" To which Johnson replied, "Why, Sir, if it be at once established that there are souls in purgatory, it is as proper to pray for them, as for our brethren of mankind who are yet in this life."[44]

And as Catholics who agree with this devout and perceptive Anglican we should never forget those souls known or unknown to us who are on the journey to God we call Purgatory. We should rejoice for them because their trials on earth are over, and they are assured of the Beatific Vision. They should be in our prayers constantly, and we should ask for their prayers as well.

As we close our discussion of Purgatory, it is appropriate to meditate on words written by Pope Benedict XVI in *Spe Salve*. Here the pope returns to the idea that the cleansing of Purgatory involves spiritual fire. He, along with some other theologians, however, envisions this fire in a way totally different from the way people did in the past. In fact, he gives us a new and far deeper understanding of the cleansing of Purgatory. His words at first may seem amazing, but as we reflect on them, we see in them the infinite love of God made manifest in Purgatory:

> Some recent theologians are of the opinion that the fire which both burns and saves is Christ himself, the Judge and Saviour. The encounter with him is the decisive act of judgment. Before his gaze all falsehood melts away. This encounter with him, as it burns us, transforms and frees us, allowing us to become truly ourselves.[45]

In these words we find a profound understanding of the doctrine of Purgatory.

Chapter Five

THE FINAL JUDGMENT AND THE
RESURRECTION OF THE BODY

"Heaven and Earth will pass away,
but my words will not pass away."

MATTHEW 24:35

The beginning of existence is shrouded in mystery. The end of existence is no less mysterious. All things in the universe — in the material world — are finite and will come to an end. Solar systems, galaxies, stars that have been around for billions of years — lengths of time too vast for the human mind to truly comprehend — will all reach an end. At some point they simply will not be.

Science wrestles with this fact, trying to understand this mysterious end point that we are all headed toward. Materialists cannot comprehend the end of the material world. Rejecting the supernatural and unable to accept anything that cannot be subjected to rational analysis, they often don't even admit the possibility of a kind of existence that is not dependent on atoms and molecules. Some even speculate about nothingness as if it were actually something. This only leads to frustration, just as do conjectures about the beginnings of material existence and the beginnings of life. At times, at a loss to explain the origins of life on our planet, some scientists have actually suggested that it may have arrived from some source outside our world or even our solar system, from worlds far away. But this solves no problems, for then they are immediately confronted with another question: How did it arise on those worlds?

All this is a desperate attempt to avoid the mystery that is inherent in both our beginning and our end. As we have seen, however, the truly great scientific minds are not uncomfortable with mystery. A scientist of the caliber of the great Albert Einstein accepted and was fascinated by mystery; unlike many of his colleagues, he was able to rise above the obviously fallacious idea that the human mind can comprehend all things.

Like Einstein, we accept and revere mystery, and as we look to examine as best we can the end of our physical world, we must remember that much is concealed from our gaze, that most of what we do know comes to us as symbols and seeming paradoxes. It is a mystery.

We look first of all at the inspired teachings of the Holy Spirit, which we find in sacred Scripture. Here we discover indications about the beginning and end of existence in our world. Naturally this knowledge is given in images that are not meant to be taken literally but to represent things that we cannot comprehend directly, things unlike anything our limited mind has encountered. Rarely does Scripture use concepts that can be said to come from the scientific vocabulary.

The descriptions of the end of the world are given in a large number of places, including the words of Christ in the Gospels, of course, but most especially in the Apocalypse, often called the Book of Revelation. It is here that we encounter difficult writings that tell us of the end of human existence, of the material world as we know it. It is very wise to ponder these words, to read them slowly and prayerfully, not to jump to conclusions about them, but to read them always with the mind of the Church. They are in fact the best thing we have available to us that takes us beyond the scientific view of the end of existence into the spiritual view, a holy view.

What we do know is that whenever the end comes, whether it is the end of the cosmos or simply the end of the earth, or the solar system, or the galaxy, it is going to happen. As we said, the nature of all material things is to rise and fall. What is now once was not; what is now will someday no longer be. This is a staggering and sobering thought, an uncomfortable idea that most people like to avoid, but the awareness of such an end is good; it should put our lives, which are so often obsessed with trivialities and nonsense, into perspective. One thing it should not do, however, is to overly distress Christians. We must never forget that people are different from the rest of the universe. Endowed with a soul, each of us is made in the image and likeness of God, and our physical end does not mean the conclusion of our lives. When all else has ceased to exist, humankind will continue to be, and we will be facing the Last Judgment.

The Last Judgment actually means the judgment of all human beings. All those made in the divine image from the beginning of humankind to its end will stand together in some unknown way facing the unfathomable mystery of God's mercy and justice. All will be revealed; the time of secrets and excuses will be past. We will be at the point of no return. But what can the Last Judgment possibly mean? How can the human mind comprehend it? We are talking about billions of people, each one created for eternal happiness with God, each one passing before the judgment seat of God, the young and the old, the good and the bad, the innocent and the guilty. The Church unambiguously tells us that they will all pass before God and be assigned a place for eternity, a place of eternal joy in the divine presence or a place of eternal separation from God — eternal emptiness, horrible, unending loss. The Last Judgment is implied — mandated — by the fact that all human beings have an immortal — or undying — element that we call the soul. This means that everyone goes to that judgment, from those who entered eternity while still embryonic children to those who died at great age. All are assigned to their ultimate eternal destiny.

It is not wise to try to get too precise in this type of thought. It is more than enough to know that judgment before God is our destiny, a mysterious destiny that cannot be fully imagined or understood in this life. Scripture gives us hints and symbols, but even these lead often to more questions, more mystery. One of the best known of these is found in the Book of the Apocalypse, a single passage that refers to the place of Armageddon as the scene of the final battle between good and evil and the judgment of all mankind.[46] This passage has given rise to much speculation over many years, and with good reason.

I remember once in the Holy Land seeing a sign in the shape of an arrow along a road. It said: "Armageddon, 4 kilometers." If ever there was a sign that made you wonder whether you wanted to continue down a road, this was it. But I did make that journey of four kilometers and saw the ruins of an ancient village deep in the valley of Jezreel. This place, Armageddon — or, more properly in Hebrew, *Har-magedon* — is steeped in history. Armageddon was the location of many decisive battles in the history of ancient Israel; it was a scene of bloodbaths. It was here that in the midst of bloody warfare the people of Israel must have thought that they were being judged by God. If their forces won, they would prosper; if they lost, destruction and perhaps slavery might be their lot. For this reason, I imagine, Armageddon is the place symbolically given us as the location of the final battle and the Last Judgment in Scripture. When you stand there at the edge of the mountains and look down at Armageddon, you behold a breathtaking scene: a huge flat plain in a valley surrounded by high mountains. Everything is bathed in intense, almost overwhelming sunlight, and the plain seems immense, unending. One could easily imagine huge armies meeting here in mortal combat, and just as easily one could envision countless people standing in this great valley, each awaiting judgment, the faults and failings of each one about to be exposed in the bright sunlight from which there is no escape.

Again, we must be careful not to interpret this literally. Armageddon, as dramatic as it may seem, is certainly not the literal place where the Last Judgment will take place, nor is it the place where good and evil will meet in final battle. Remember, all this will happen after the end, when our physical world no longer exists. Probably there is no place on our planet that could hold the throngs of people who would await their destiny before the throne of God.

We all are tempted to turn our imagination in the direction of the great gathering or "assizes" (a word used in medieval times for a place in which everyone accused in a specific area would be judged by the local ruler). This may be a helpful metaphor, but we must understand that it remains a metaphor, a way of speaking about something for which we have no words. The mysterious judgment of God in no way resembles any courtroom that anyone has seen. The judgment of God is carried out in perfect justice, perfect knowledge, and perfect mercy, and all verdicts are final ones. In the Last Judgment there can be no errors or extenuating circumstances. Somehow or other, in a way we cannot begin to imagine, each person passes before God, the Creator and Judge, and each receives exactly the judgment his earthly choices have merited him.

I have attempted to live a religious life as devoutly as I could, but I would not for one minute think of presenting myself as innocent at the Last Judgment. No one can. Those who in this world declare themselves sinless will find their inner truths revealed at the Last Judgment and will realize they have nothing left to depend on but the Divine Mercy. I am sure there will be many who will feel rather foolish as they look back on their estimation of their virtues and rewards. Scripture tells us to look for the mercy of God, and the Church reminds of this constantly, for without it we would surely be lost. As I imagine the Last Judgment, I picture the saints, still aware of their own earthly foibles, singing over and over again in chorus: "Lord, have mercy. Lord, have mercy. Lord, have mercy."

The Second Coming of Christ

"He will come again in glory to judge the living and the dead." These are words we repeat often at Mass during the Nicene Creed, the Profession of Faith, and they are words that have stirred the imagination of countless Christians for many centuries. We know them to be true; they come to us as part of the deposit of faith, but we have no idea when the truth contained in these few words will come to pass. When will Jesus come? No one can ever answer that question, for only God has that knowledge. Emphatically, our Savior tells us: "But of that day and hour no one knows, not even the angels of heaven, nor the Son, but the Father only" (Matthew 24:36).

Unfortunately, over the centuries these very unambiguous biblical words have not stopped people from speculating, nor have they stopped people from attempting to devise ways to determine the date of the end of the world, the Second Coming of Christ, and the Last Judgment. Many Protestant groups such as the Seventh-day Adventists and the Jehovah's Witnesses have made definite predictions, which fortunately or unfortunately (depending on your point of view) did not take place. Presumably both groups were disappointed when they got out of bed on the morning after the day on which the world was supposed to end.

The fascination with the Second Coming of Christ is usually paired with a belief in millennialism, the assertion that the coming of Christ will be in two stages: The first will begin with the great battle of Armageddon, the cataclysmic conflict between good and evil in which Christ will destroy the Antichrist. This will be followed by a thousand-year-long reign of Christ on earth — an earth peopled now only by the virtuous and pure. Yet another cataclysm will then occur, a great struggle in which Satan is defeated forever; it is this that leads to the Final Judgment.

The Church, along with most traditional Christian bodies, rejects such teachings, which come from a too-literal reading of the Book of the Apocalypse, and maintains that Christ's words in the Gospel of Matthew are to be believed, that the end of time will occur at a moment and in a way we can never know.

The ideas of millennialism may be hard for the average Catholic to grasp. Part of the reason for this may be that despite our conflicts in the Middle East and several other parts of the world, we are at comparative peace. When we rise in the morning, we do not fear destruction and chaos; we are relatively assured that we and our loved ones will be okay once bedtime rolls around again. But this was not always the case. Only a few decades ago, a time certainly within the memories of at least some of my readers, there was no shortage of candidates for the Antichrist. The horrors of World War II, the uncertainty of the future, and the presence of evil on an immense scale, capable of seemingly endless and senseless devastation, were with us all. At that time and for some years afterward many people, including many clergy, saw things that they very understandably interpreted as signs of the end of the world. How can you blame them at such a time? Who can be criticized for wondering whether Adolph Hitler or Joseph Stalin might actually be the Antichrist?

A preoccupation with the end of the world and the Second Coming of Christ has reasserted itself over and over again throughout history. Saint Bernardine of Siena, a fifteenth-century Franciscan, became so frustrated with people's concern about this that he is said to have exclaimed that he had heard much of the second coming of Jesus, but that Jesus had not yet come so it might be better for people to lead a Christian life.

Like Saint Bernardine we should concentrate on our present lives, our relations to others, and especially our relationship to Christ rather than looking forward to end-of-the-world fireworks. We must also not lose sight of the fact that at the moment of our death our fate is sealed. Our personal death and our personal judgment are what should concern us greatly, for the Last Judgment, despite its enormity and finality, will not change our destiny. Final Judgment brings creation to its full completion, irrevocably separating the good from the evil. The good are thus finally able to experience the fullness of goodness in glorified body and soul, not just as individuals but as a vibrant and everlasting human community of perfect love that — together with the angels — is united completely to God. The blessed will no longer be burdened by the damned in their midst. In the Final Judgment the community of the damned is also brought to full completion in an everlasting experience of the consequence of their sins in both resurrected body and soul. As the saved will exist in perfect peace, the damned will exist in perpetual turmoil and despair.

The individual judgment remains a personal experience. The Final Judgment includes all humankind from Adam onward and brings humanity to its ultimate completion.[47] Therefore, it is how we live our lives now that will bring us to everlasting joy or eternal emptiness. The Last Judgment will bring creation to its full richness and color. It will certainly be an interesting experience, and I'm definitely hoping to get a good seat — but it will not be a time of surprises if you read the Gospel.

The Hope of Judgment

While speculation about the end of the world has abounded throughout the history of Christianity, the modern person — even the modern Christian — may live as if there is no Last Judgment. A sense of some kind of Final Judgment is a characteristic of most religious people and cultures and has been so since the dawn of humankind. The fact that we now lack this tells us much about our contemporary civilization. In my estimation it shows that we are losing touch more and more with the realities of our lives, with the ground of our existence, with the very idea of transcendence. We have somehow forgotten to look ahead! In a sense, life without a Final Judgment becomes incomplete, absurd. Such a judgment is necessary if our lives are to have meaning, if our sufferings are not to be in vain. If there is no Final Judgment, what distinguishes the monstrously cruel from their victims? How can we claim that our lives have true dignity if we are ultimately held accountable for nothing? In a way, those who deny the Last Judgment have subtly denied the existence of God, as well, at least the God of Abraham, Isaac, and Jacob, the God and Father of our Lord Jesus Christ. Pope Benedict XVI in his encyclical *Spe Salvi* discusses this extensively. In the face of the denial of theism and of God's justice the pope tells us:

God has given himself an "image": in Christ who was made man. In him who was crucified, the denial of false images of God is taken to an extreme. God now reveals his true face in the figure of the sufferer who shares man's God-forsaken condition by taking it upon himself. This innocent sufferer has attained the certitude of hope: there is a God, and God can create justice in a way that we cannot conceive, yet we can begin to grasp it through faith. Yes, there is a resurrection of the flesh. There is justice. There is an "undoing" of past suffering, a reparation that sets things aright. For this reason, faith in the Last Judgment is first and foremost hope — the need for which was made abundantly clear in the upheavals of recent centuries. I am convinced that the question of justice constitutes the essential argument, or in any case the strongest argument, in favor of faith in eternal life. The purely individual need for a fulfillment that is denied to us in this life, for an everlasting love that we await, is certainly an important motive for believing that man was made for eternity; but only in connection with the impossibility that the injustice of history should be the final word does the necessity for Christ's return and for new life become fully convincing.[48]

In Pope Benedict's words we find a mature understanding of the Last Judgment, one that is profoundly and truthfully Christian. Here we are made to see that in the Last Judgment the value of our humanity will be affirmed in a unique way. In the Last Judgment God's justice rights the untold wrongs of human history, undoes the victimhood of the victims, and obliterates the seeming triumphs of sinners over others. In the Last Judgment we encounter not only God as a stern judge before whom we tremble in fear and awe, but also as the God who binds our wounds, who offers us ultimate solace and hope, who transforms the difficult trials of our lives into pathways to joy.

The End of the World in the Light of the Resurrection

Thus far we have looked at the Church's teaching on the Last Judgment in general. Now we shall examine some ramifications of these teachings. The Church has always taught that the body will be resurrected; in this she has never wavered, nor will she ever. In *Spe Salvi* Pope Benedict XVI makes it very clear that the resurrection of the flesh is an essential part of God's plan for us. This means that at the end of the ages all human beings will be resurrected, their bodies and souls coming together in a way that is more perfectly united than we can presently understand.

Of course this belief in both resurrection and judgment is not unique to us; it was held by our Jewish ancestors in faith, the first to hear the word of God. We have but to open the Hebrew Bible to the Book of Daniel to read: "Many of those who sleep in the dust of the earth shall awake; some shall live forever, others shall be an everlasting horror and disgrace. But the wise shall shine brightly like the splendor of the firmament, And those who lead the many to justice shall be like the stars forever" (Daniel 12: 2-3). This Jewish belief, which was preserved by the Pharisees after the destruction of the Temple in A.D. 70, continues into the present. To this very day every traditional Jewish liturgy contains the following prayer, which powerfully affirms God's resurrection of the dead:

> Lord who art mighty for all eternity, Thou revivest the dead, Thou upholdest the falling. Thou healest the sick. Thou freest the bound, keeping faith with those who sleep in the dust. Who is like Thee, Lord of power! Who can be compared with thee, King who sends death and gives life, and causes His saving power to flourish! Thou wilt keep faith in reviving the dead. Blessed art Thou, Lord who revives the dead.[49]

The words of Christ are our best proof of the coming resurrection of the dead. He spoke most forcefully about it in his debate with the Sadducees who, unlike the Pharisees, denied resurrection. We find this recorded in the Gospel of Saint Matthew:

> The same day Sadducees came to him, who say that there is no resurrection; and they asked him a question, saying, "Teacher, Moses said, 'If a man dies, having no children, his brother must marry the widow, and raise up children for his brother.' Now there were seven brothers among us; the first married, and died, and having no children left his wife to his brother. So too the second and third, down to the seventh. After them all, the woman died. In the resurrection, therefore, to which of the seven will she be wife? For they all had her." But Jesus answered them, "You are wrong, because you know neither the scriptures nor the power of God. For in the resurrection they neither marry nor are given in marriage, but are like angels in heaven. And as for the resurrection of the dead, have you not read what was said to you by God, 'I am the God of Abraham, and the God of Isaac, and the God of Jacob'? He is not God of the dead, but of the living." And when the crowd heard it, they were astonished at his teaching. (Matthew 22:23-33)

The resurrection is proclaimed throughout the New Testament, most forcefully by Saint Paul. In fact, sections of his First Letter to the Corinthians are a profound meditation on the resurrection of the body. In this beautiful epistle, Saint Paul writes:

Now if Christ is preached as raised from the dead, how can some of you say that there is no resurrection of the dead? But if there is no resurrection of the dead, then Christ has not been raised; if Christ has not been raised, then our preaching is in vain and your faith is in vain. We are even found to be misrepresenting God, because we testified of God that he raised Christ, whom he did not raise if it is true that the dead are not raised. For if the dead are not raised, then Christ has not been raised. If Christ has not been raised, your faith is futile and you are still in your sins. Then those also who have fallen asleep in Christ have perished. If for this life only we have hoped in Christ, we are of all men most to be pitied. (1 Corinthians 15:12-19)

Later, the same epistle becomes almost a hymn to the resurrection of the body and to God's great mercy in granting us eternal life: "What is sown is perishable," writes Saint Paul, "what is raised is imperishable. It is sown in dishonor, it is raised in glory. It is sown in weakness, it is raised in power. It is sown a physical body, it is raised a spiritual body. If there is a physical body, there is also a spiritual body. Thus it is written, 'the first man Adam became a living being'; the last Adam became a life-giving spirit." (1 Corinthians 15:42-45).

As his meditation of the resurrection concludes, the words of Saint Paul take on a tone of joy, of unquenchable hope as he says: "When the perishable puts on the imperishable, and the mortal puts on immortality, then shall come to pass the saying that is written: 'Death is swallowed up in victory.' 'O death, where is thy victory? O death, where is thy sting?' " (1 Corinthians 15: 54-55).

Resurrection was the fervent belief of the early Church. The idea that the body would be reunited with the soul after the Last Judgment into a self that far transcends the selves we are now in this mortal life animated the faith of the Church Fathers. It was at the very core of the Church's understanding of God's love for us all. The early Church Fathers proclaimed this without hesitation, among them Saint Augustine, who was deeply inspired by Saint Paul's First Epistle to the Corinthians and wrote:

Therefore God will bestow a wonderful facility, a wonderful lightness. Not without cause are those bodies called spiritual. They are not called spiritual because they will be spirits and not bodies. The bodies we now have are called "souled" bodies and yet they are not souls but bodies. As they are now said to be "souled" and yet are not souls, so they will then be called spiritual but not be spirits, because they will be bodies. Why therefore, dearly beloved is it called spiritual body except for the fact that it will serve at the spirit's pleasure? Nothing of yourself will contradict yourself, nothing in you will rebel against you.[50]

The Book of the Apocalypse is certainly among the most difficult books of the Bible. Filled with obscure symbols and frightening occurrences, it is so difficult to understand that many people find it impenetrable. Yet it is the book of the Apocalypse to which we turn when we try to understand the Last Judgment, for it is also filled with beautiful poetry and images of the Last Judgment that speak of hope and joy, mysterious symbols that we do not quite understand but that renew our faith in the God who has redeemed us from death in Christ and who will temper his justice with mercy when we stand before him:

... a great multitude which no man could number, from every nation, from all tribes and peoples and tongues, standing before the throne and before the Lamb, clothed in white robes, with palm branches in their hands, and crying out with a loud voice, "Salvation belongs to our God who sits upon the throne, and to the Lamb!" And all the angels stood round the throne and round the elders and the four living creatures, and they fell on their faces before the throne and worshiped God, saying, "Amen! Blessing and glory and wisdom and thanksgiving and honor and power and might be to our God for ever and ever! Amen." (Apocalypse 7:9-12)

Chapter Six

ETERNAL LIFE

*"Christ is risen from the dead, trampling down death by death,
and upon those in the tombs bestowing life."*

PASCHAL TROPARION[51]

PART I: WORDS OF LIFE

The words that Christ speaks in the Gospel are words of life. They are certainly the most important words given to us or to any human being past or present. Often Christ's words are difficult; they make us confront the fact that we are less than we like to think we are. Christ's words to us are mysterious and call us to ponder things we cannot fully know or comprehend, that we must work hard simply to sense. I have attempted to read these words carefully and solemnly, to meditate on them regularly and with an open heart over many years. I have no doubt that many of the people reading this book have done no less. Such people are well aware that the words of Christ confront us in ways no other words can and have done so since the beginning of our awareness of the world around us. They return to us over and over again in different contexts, and they probably became part of our lives even before we could understand their origin or anything about their meaning. Before we ever sat down to read even a small passage of the Gospel, bits and pieces of it were read to us, often by our parents or grandparents. Sometimes they read to us from inscriptions on the walls of churches, at other times from holy cards or parts of prayers. Of course we have regularly heard these words spoken by a priest at every Mass we have ever attended.

These are, therefore, familiar words, sometimes so familiar that we may lose a sense of their importance, their utter uniqueness. Often, paradoxically, it is the convert to the faith, the one to whom these words are new, who experiences a startling aware-ness of the power inherent in them. But sometimes we are able to glimpse their great meaning — their extraordinary significance — for an instant or two. Sometimes we see Christ's words for what they really are, and they become like lightning, brilliantly illumi-nating the darkness in which we walk.

We have already spoken of Purgatory, Hell, and judgment. All these discussions have had to depend on language that is symbolic, metaphorical. These realities exceed our experience so completely that we cannot approach them directly but only obliquely, letting the things we do understand represent and suggest the things that we don't. When it comes to the eternal life that we call Heaven, we are on even shakier ground, for who can imagine what it must be to be in the presence of God? Eternal life is more than anything we know. It is something that surpasses our earthly experience so completely that when we try to understand it, our imagination will fail us. It is more difficult for us to picture eternal life than it is for one born blind to imagine what red or blue or green might mean. Therefore we do not turn to our imagination or to "our frail and feeble minds" when contemplating such mysteries. All our own words may fail us, but there are some words that can never fail us, and these are the words that we shall use to look at eternal life — the words of Christ.

It is in the words of Christ that we find eternal life, and I would like to share with my readers some of these words that are most meaningful to me, that are most revealing. To me these words offer enormous hope and point us toward mysteries that we cannot comprehend but on which we can stake our lives. They are the words uttered by our Divine Redeemer at the Last Supper. They form part of the long sermon He gave to His Apostles on that mysterious night that brought the Holy Eucharist into being, that night that preceded His Passion and death by only a few short hours. These are the words spoken by Christ before He made the great sacrifice that was destined to alter the world forever — to offer man eternity rather than a brief moment in time.

Saint John the Evangelist records for us Christ's precious words in chapters 14 through 17 of his Gospel. These pages are often called the "Book of Glory," and rightly so. Within this section of the Gospel I want to focus first on words that are of unique importance to me and to us all: the words found in John 14:1-7. I wish that every Christian would memorize and recite them often and contemplate them prayerfully at every significant moment, for these words are the "gates of heaven":

> Let not your hearts be troubled; believe in God, believe also in me. In my Father's house are many rooms; if it were not so, would I have told you that I go to prepare a place for you? And when I go and prepare a place for you, I will come again and will take you to myself, that where I am you may be also. And you know the way where I am going." Thomas said to him, "Lord, we do not know where you are going; how can we know the way?" Jesus said to him, "I am the way, and the truth, and the life; no one comes to the Father, but by me. If you had known me, you would have known my Father also; henceforth you know him and have seen him." (John 14:1-7)

These words that Christ spoke to His followers at the Last Supper are simultaneously the promise of eternal joy in our heavenly Father's home and the preparation for the horrible torture and life-giving death of His Son. It is necessary to meditate on these incredible words before one is able to perceive what is truly being promised in them. Here we have the most mysterious events in human history being played out before us — events that transcend every other mystery. As we meditate on them, we discover ourselves immersed in horror and death, in failure and desolation — it is as if we are drowning. But we find we are soon brought with Christ out of the depths to everlasting hope and to something almost too exalted for us to imagine: life eternal for sinful man.

Life eternal: This is a thought beyond the comprehension of creatures who live in our dying world. It is a possibility beyond all human hope, and it is offered to us despite the fact that even the best of us — the great saints among us — can never be worthy of it. Through the death and Resurrection of Jesus, something that by rights belongs to God alone is given to us, the very ones who spend our days on earth committing one sin after another, offending our heavenly Father in every way.

But what is this incredible gift? Of what can it consist? Our human minds, so cluttered with day-to-day foolishness, barely think of it. When we do, we usually imagine a world somewhat like the one we now inhabit but without unhappiness, a world of tranquility — a rather boring world. Perhaps we think of a misty existence in which nothing has much substance. But eternal life is finally to have the most substance, to be at last the beings that God created us to be before the Fall of man, to be whole in every respect, to be beyond all harm and in the presence of God, to know the One who is the source of all things, to experience the Beatific Vision. Eternal life — Heaven — usually a superficial, hazy thought at the edge of our consciousness until a tragedy shocks us out of our complacency and forces us to think of it, should not be a vague concept at all. It is reality at its purest; it is the overwhelming presence of God, of eternal and infinite love.

We seldom think of where the dead are now in their reality — their being. Perhaps such thoughts cross our minds about a saint if we're at his tomb or perhaps on his feast day, but we rarely think such thoughts concerning anyone else. We hope for those we love but somehow seem unable to imagine anything about their present reality. The world abets this confusion by trying to create its own heavens, but these become sad mockeries. The tomb of Lenin in Red Square is one such attempt. It is ghoulish and gloomy. In it Lenin's corpse has been refrigerated and preserved for decades. This is a sign of the rejection of eternal life; it is an embrace of death, of everlasting nothingness, a desperate attempt to cling to the remnants of this earthly life when such life has already ended.

Human beings can be ridiculous when faced with thoughts of eternity. Even the best-intentioned person will show little or no depth when it comes to contemplating eternal life. I once presided over the funeral of a poor fellow who had drunk himself to death, a man who had little connection with religion, but whose family wanted a religious funeral. As we lowered the casket into the ground a number of his drinking buddies (and there were quite a few) expressed sentiments to me such as the following — in all sincerity: "I hope you guys [the clergy] are right about the man upstairs." I've always thought that God has a sense of humor; for the sake of people such as these, I hope so.

Facing Death and Life

It is important that we contemplate our own reactions to death and to that great and mysterious reality that transcends it, the reality we call eternal life. For the believer, the promise of eternal life is the greatest of all hopes. It is this great promise that endows our earthly life with its meaning and robs our physical death of its power. We must never forget this. In fact, the Christian should never even think of physical death alone but always in conjunction with eternal life. For us it should be as if these two mysteries are each halves of the same whole, two sides of the same coin; they should be as inseparable in our minds as they are in God's plan of redemption for us. This is essential, for death considered alone is a sorrow; in fact, it can even be a horror. Death alone — without the possibility of eternal life — is an irrevocable end. Such an ending is the way the world sees death; it cannot be the way the Christian sees death. I am reminded of words written by Saint John Vianney in this regard: "The eyes of the world see no further than this life . . . but the eyes of the Christian see deep into eternity." We must be true Christians and see into eternity. We must never forget that death comes to us bearing the promise of renewed and unending life. The thought of life after death is a very serious part of our awareness, of our own self-concept. It tells us a great deal about what we think of ourselves.

We approach this great mystery in humble prayer and meditation. This is the only way we can begin to glimpse something of a reality that is beyond our powers to understand fully, to prayerfully consider Christ's promise of eternal life, to contemplate over and over again the great reality that lies behind this promise and comes to us as the ultimate expression of the love of God.

Life after death and the promise of eternal life should fill us with awe every time we think of them. Yet they should be realities with which the Christian lives at every moment. We are people whose every action should be taken in the light of eternity, for it is eternity that gives our actions their value and our lives their meaning. Without eternal life our earthly lives are reduced to sad mysteries — pointless mysteries that are constantly fading into nothingness. As we contemplate this, we become aware that we can hope to know only a tiny fraction of what awaits us. These fragments — these glimpses — are given to us in the Scriptures, especially in Christ's own words. Only He knows the reality of eternal life because He alone has come from the Father. He tells us:

> I am the bread of life; he who comes to me shall not hunger, and he who believes in me shall never thirst. But I said to you that you have seen me and yet do not believe. All that the Father gives me will come to me; and him who comes to me I will not cast out. For I have come down from heaven, not to do my own will, but the will of him who sent me; and this is the will of him who sent me, that I should lose nothing of all that he has given me, but raise it up at the last day. For this is the will of my Father, that every one who sees the Son and believes in him should have eternal life; and I will raise him up at the last day. (John 6:35-40)

We are not alone in our difficulty in finding ways to react to these and other words of Jesus. Even spiritual giants struggle. Saint Paul was very sensitive to the meaning behind Christ's words. He also obviously had a very practical approach to theology (he wanted things to happen!), yet he was well aware that the promise of eternal life was profoundly mysterious. When he tries to speak of it he stumbles: "What no eye has seen, nor ear heard, nor the heart of man conceived, what God has prepared for those who love him" (1 Corinthians 2:9), he says, echoing Isaiah 64:4, as if this articulate and inspired man cannot find words to express what this great promise entails. However, immediately after this Saint Paul tells us that the Holy Spirit searches everything, including even in the depths of God and the thoughts of God:

> ... the Spirit searches everything, even the depths of God. For what person knows a man's thoughts except the spirit

of the man which is in him? So also no one comprehends the thoughts of God except the Spirit of God. Now we have received not the spirit of the world, but the Spirit which is from God, that we might understand the gifts bestowed on us by God. And we impart this in words not taught by human wisdom but taught by the Spirit, interpreting spiritual truths to those who possess the Spirit. (1 Corinthians 2:10-13)

In these words and those that follow Saint Paul makes a most emphatic demand that one must be sensitive to the movements of the Holy Spirit, who knows all things, even the very depths of God. By accepting the Holy Spirit into our lives, we open ourselves to knowledge that is otherwise unknowable. With the help of the Spirit, we are able to see these mysteries through spiritual eyes rather than eyes that are dulled and clouded by our mundane existence. Think of what love this shows: God allows our small and terribly finite human minds to understand a bit of how He actually looks at us: this is the marvel of grace! In all this we see what man must do to begin to be worthy of the promises of Christ, of eternal life. He cannot depend upon himself but must allow the Holy Spirit to enlighten him — to give him the gift of seeing as God sees. It is thus that we may enter the "mind of Christ."

Saint Paul's words are powerful, but they are not enough. He knows them to be inadequate and uses them to point us back to other words: again the words of Christ. If we are to approach the words of our divine Savior in the Gospels, Paul makes it plain that we must first take stock of ourselves, transform ourselves. We must ask ourselves what these words mean for us. Under the gracious guidance of the Holy Spirit we must search our minds, as Saint Paul says "the spirit searches everything," asking ourselves whether we have truly accepted the teachings of Christ that we encounter in the Gospels, or whether we have we satisfied ourselves with some pale imitation of them. Have we — like so many — attempted to empty them of the great meaning they contain, to tame them, to make them speak of things we can grasp rather than things we must accept?

We must also be sure that we understand, as best we can, not just the words of Christ but the whole body of Christ's teachings that come to us not in His own direct words but sometimes through the Apostles and the very early Church. The Church is the bearer of Christ's teachings, as well as their guard and interpreter, and this is something we must not forget. We Christians first of all must love Christ and believe that we are loved by the Father, for Christ tells us that love forms the basis for the existence of eternal life: "If a man loves me, he will keep my word, and my Father will love him, and we will come to him and make our home with him" says Jesus in the Gospel of Saint John (John 14:23). Christ then promises that the Holy Spirit will be sent by the Father: "But the Counselor, the Holy Spirit, whom the Father will send in my name, he will teach you all things, and bring to your remembrance all that I have said to you" (John 14:26). In these words we find the Father and the Son working through the Holy Spirit, the Holy Trinity acting to bring us to eternal life. We also find here our duty and our joy-filled future. We must do our part; we must strive to understand as best we can the words of Christ and struggle to keep them every day of our lives. If we do this, the Father, the Son, and with them the Holy Spirit will dwell in us, will fill us to overflowing with their eternity, will bring us to the eternal life that by rights is God's alone.

Skepticism and Faith

All that I have written about is likely to be foreign to the contemporary mind. It is mystical, and mysticism is something we don't care very much about today. It's something we have a hard time understanding. Therefore it is extremely important in the present situation, when faith has been so often weakened or even replaced by skepticism — a skepticism that is filling the Christian world — that we again make certain we know what we really believe. If we are not certain, the concept of eternal life is likely to become meaningless for us; it will seem mythological, magical, a fairytale that contemporary people have outgrown.

Pope Benedict XVI himself has spoken about this in his book *Jesus of Nazareth*[52] and pointed out the many attempts made over the last several decades to make the "historical life" of Jesus the only thing we know about Christ, to reduce all things to mere human attempts to understand history. This has been a concerted effort to deny anything that "our frail and feeble minds" cannot grasp. And it has left us with an uncertain and diminished faith. It has made us uneasy with concepts such as eternal life and the resurrection of the body. Pope Benedict has pointed out that this procedure, this way of looking at Christ, has made Him seem more and more distant from us, and it has destroyed the possibility of devotion to Christ, which the pope identifies as the essential part of Christian life. If Christ is distant and Christ is the one who brings us to eternal life, then eternal life, too, must be distant, perhaps a figment of the imagination, a lovely myth among a million lovely myths.

When we come to the question of eternal life, therefore, it is utterly, absolutely necessary that we proceed in faith and with the scriptural teaching of the words of Christ and of the New Testament writers, particularly Saint Paul and the writer of the Apocalypse. If one does not read these words through the eyes of faith, but turns them into nothing more than another text to be studied and analyzed (as contemporary skeptics would have us do), the understanding of eternal life will elude us. Holy Scripture is God's conversation with us, not simply the sharing of the limited thoughts of men. We must read these words to understand the "mind of Christ." If we do not, we will have closed our minds and our souls to the mystery of eternal life. Many have already done this.

It can honestly be said at the present time that there are people who claim to be Christians whose own belief has been so undermined that they have no real expectation of eternal life. They may have some vague sort of hunch, a feeling really. They imagine something that resembles a generalized world soul that transcends this world and this life. Perhaps it is similar to Nirvana, a concept common in many Eastern religions in which everything is finally absorbed into an ultimate and abstract reality. Such people have lost the faith that enables them to assent to Christ's promises. They can no longer dare to believe that our God is not some impersonal "ground of being" but our loving Father. To such people the concept of the individual surviving in eternal life has been discarded. To the Christian, however, it can never be discarded. It is our hope. It is our certainty. It is what gives our lives meaning.

Christ's Promise of Eternal Life

In several places in the Gospels, Jesus speaks very directly of eternal life and the Kingdom of God. Perhaps the most obvious are those words said by Christ almost immediately before His Passion and death. This is the parable in the Gospel of Saint Matthew of the Last Judgment, which identifies those who are willing to be generous with those in desperate need. Christ says:

> "When the Son of man comes in his glory, and all the angels with him, then he will sit on his glorious throne. Before him will be gathered all the nations, and he will separate them one from another as a shepherd separates the sheep from the goats, and he will place the sheep at his right hand, but the goats at the left. Then the King will say to those at his right hand, 'Come, O blessed of my Father, inherit the kingdom prepared for you from the foundation of the world.' " (Matthew 25:31-34)

In the nineteenth chapter of the Gospel of Saint Matthew, Peter asks of Christ: "Lo, we have left everything and followed you. What then shall we have?" Jesus responds, "Truly, I say to you, in the new world, when the Son of man shall sit on his glorious throne, you who have followed me will also sit on twelve thrones, judging the twelve tribes of Israel" (Matthew 19:27-28).

In Saint Matthew's Gospel, parables are used to denote eternal life. One of these is the parable of the weeds. Here Christ speaks of weeds that have grown up in a field, choking out the wheat that has been planted there. Christ explains this parable by saying:

> "He who sows the good seed is the Son of man; the field is the world, and the good seed means the sons of the kingdom; the weeds are the sons of the evil one, and the enemy

who sowed them is the devil; the harvest is the close of the age, and the reapers are angels. Just as the weeds are gathered and burned with fire, so will it be at the close of the age. The Son of man will send his angels, and they will gather out of his kingdom all causes of sin and all evildoers, and throw them into the furnace of fire; there men will weep and gnash their teeth. Then the righteous will shine like the sun in the kingdom of their Father." (Matthew 13:37-43)

Often in the Gospel of Saint Matthew, Christ refers to eternal life in ways that are threatening to people who do evil things. He tells people that to enter into eternal life, they must change their ways drastically: "Not every one who says to me, 'Lord, Lord,' shall enter the kingdom of heaven, but he who does the will of my Father who is in heaven" (Matthew 7:21). This reminds us once again of the precariousness of our situation. Eternal life can be ours, but we must not take it for granted. We must do the will of the Father. We must make real in our lives those difficult words we confront in the prayer that Jesus taught us: "Thy will be done." We say these words often with our lips, but in our hearts are we not really saying, "My will be done?"

During the Sermon on the Mount, Christ tells all who will follow him: "Blessed are you when men revile you and persecute you and utter all kinds of evil against you falsely on my account. Rejoice and be glad, for your reward is great in heaven, for so men persecuted the prophets who were before you" (Matthew 5:11-12). Here we see once again how the will of the Father is different from the will of the world — from our will. Following the will of the Father can be difficult; it can even make us outcasts. But by so doing, by struggling to obey God rather than our own selfish desires, we allow eternity to be revealed in our lives even now. We permit God to lead us from this dying world to a world that can never die.

In the thirteenth chapter of the Gospel of Saint Luke, Christ tells the parable of the narrow gate, warning people that it is not always easy to enter the Kingdom of God, and He warns that those who appear to be last may actually be first. He also uses the parable of the rich man and Lazarus, and says of Lazarus the beggar that he is in the bosom of Abraham after death, an expression that speaks clearly of reward after death, of rest, of acceptance.

In the Gospel of Saint John very clear indications are given of eternal life. In Jesus' conversation with Nicodemus we read these famous words: "For God so loved the world that he gave his only Son, that whoever believes in him should not perish but have eternal life" (John 3:16). And in the next chapter, Christ promises the Samaritan woman at the well: "Every one who drinks of this water will thirst again, but whoever drinks of the water that I shall give him will never thirst; the water that I shall give him will become in him a spring of water welling up to eternal life" (John 4:13-14).

In an argument with His adversaries, Jesus says:

> "... the hour is coming, and now is, when the dead will hear the voice of the Son of God, and those who hear will live. For as the Father has life in himself, so he has granted the Son also to have life in himself, and has given him authority to execute judgment, because he is the Son of man. Do not marvel at this; for the hour is coming when all who are in the tombs will hear his voice and come forth, those who have done good, to the resurrection of life, and those who have done evil, to the resurrection of judgment." (John 5:25-29)

As we have seen, there are many passages in the Gospel of Saint John in which Christ speaks explicitly of eternal life. One of the most powerful of these concerns His words on the Bread of Life, which we find in the sixth chapter of this Gospel. Jesus says:

> "Truly, truly, I say to you, it was not Moses who gave you the bread from heaven; my Father gives you the true bread from heaven. For the bread of God is that which comes down from heaven, and gives life to the world." They said to him, "Lord, give us this bread always." Jesus said to them, "I am the bread of life; he who comes to me shall not hunger, and he who believes in me shall never thirst. But

I said to you that you have seen me and yet do not believe. All that the Father gives me will come to me; and him who comes to me I will not cast out. For I have come down from heaven, not to do my own will, but the will of him who sent me; and this is the will of him who sent me, that I should lose nothing of all that he has given me, but raise it up at the last day. For this is the will of my Father, that every one who sees the Son and believes in him should have eternal life; and I will raise him up at the last day." (John 6:32-40)

The death of Lazarus and his restoration to life is an equally powerful but somewhat different revelation of eternal life, one which reminds us forcefully that we will know eternal life not as disembodied spirits but as a perfect union of soul and body, of perfected spirit and transformed matter. Jesus speaks to Martha, who is distraught at the death of her brother:

Jesus said to her, "Your brother will rise again." Martha said to him, "I know that he will rise again in the resurrection at the last day." Jesus said to her, "I am the resurrection and the life; he who believes in me, though he die, yet shall he live, and whoever lives and believes in me shall never die. Do you believe this?" She said to him, "Yes, Lord; I believe that you are the Christ, the Son of God, he who is coming into the world." (John 11:23-27)

This is an incredibly powerful statement, yet it is not the most powerful one Jesus ever made. That is a statement we have already seen, the words of Jesus that are recorded in the fourteenth chapter of the Gospel of Saint John, the first words of His that we considered at the beginning of this chapter. In these words proclaimed by Christ to His Apostles we come, as it were, to the summit of His teaching. They are elaborated and expanded on later in His prayer to His Father called the High Priestly Prayer, which is found at the beginning of the Passion according to Saint John:

When Jesus had spoken these words, he lifted up his eyes to heaven and said, "Father, the hour has come; glorify thy Son that the Son may glorify thee, since thou hast given him power over all flesh, to give eternal life to all whom thou hast given him. And this is eternal life, that they know thee the only true God, and Jesus Christ whom thou hast sent. I glorified thee on earth, having accomplished the work which thou gavest me to do; and now, Father, glorify thou me in thy own presence with the glory which I had with thee before the world was made." (John 17:1-5)

And then only a few lines later He says: "I am praying for them; I am not praying for the world but for those whom thou hast given me, for they are thine; all mine are thine, and thine are mine, and I am glorified in them" (John 17:9-10).

Christ continues speaking in a way that shows His very personal concern for his followers: "I do not pray that thou shouldst take them out of the world, but that thou shouldst keep them from the evil one. They are not of the world, even as I am not of the world. Sanctify them in the truth; thy word is truth. As thou didst send me into the world, so I have sent them into the world. And for their sake I consecrate myself, that they also may be consecrated in truth" (John 17:15-19). He then turns to all of us in the future, the hundreds of millions — in fact billions — of people who believe in him, showing that this great promise of eternal life is not restricted, but is open all of mankind: "I do not pray for these only, but also for those who believe in me through their word, that they may all be one; even as thou, Father, art in me, and I in thee, that they also may be in us, so that the world may believe that thou hast sent me" (John 17:20-21).

These precious words of hope and of promise must come to an end in the Gospels, and it is a startling end, for we realize that these words of life, these promises of unending joy that Jesus makes are the prelude to His death. We see clearly that our life is to spring from the offering of His life for us. Jesus proceeds to the Garden of Gethsemane, where He prays in agony until He is arrested and led to His death. This is, however, a death that recalls His words of life and endows them with even deeper meaning. His crucifixion is revealed as being not a moment of failure, despair, and destruction but the beginning of the ultimate work of

God, the source of new life, new hope, new being. As we contemplate it, we think as well of His Resurrection and Ascension, of His preparing a way for us to the Father.

We look at the words of Christ and know them to be far more than words. They are in some mysterious way the very thing they describe: They are eternal life. We find eternal life within them. No one can experience in this human world the full reality of eternal life. "Our frail and feeble minds" can only begin to comprehend such a reality. The Savior gives us symbols, symbols that seem to participate in the very thing they symbolize, but even our understanding of these is limited and cannot be otherwise. We think of such symbols as "Our Father's House," the "heavenly banquet," and in them we find momentary glimpses of ultimate reality — things that cannot be expressed in mere words. The inspired author of the Apocalypse seems to offer us explicit descriptions of the other world, but we must remind ourselves that here, too, we are confronted with symbols, divine metaphors for things beyond our grasp. The words and descriptions of the Apocalypse are so dramatic that we often make the mistake of assuming they are actually events in our world. These passages are very powerful for contemplation, but they are certainly not a travelogue of eternity:

> After this I heard what seemed to be the loud voice of a great multitude in heaven, crying,
>
> > "Hallelujah! Salvation and glory and power belong to
> > our God, for his judgments are true and just;
> > he has judged the great harlot who corrupted the earth
> > with her fornication,
> > and he has avenged on her the blood of his servants."
>
> Once more they cried,
>
> > "Hallelujah! The smoke from her goes up for ever and
> > ever."
>
> And the twenty-four elders and the four living creatures
> fell down and worshiped God who is seated on the throne,

saying, "Amen. Hallelujah!" And from the throne came a voice crying,

> "Praise our God, all you his servants,
> you who fear him, small and great."

Then I heard what seemed to be the voice of a great multitude, like the sound of many waters and like the sound of mighty thunderpeals, crying,

> "Hallelujah! For the Lord our God the Almighty
> reigns." (Apocalypse 19:1-6)

And then a little further on we find words of incredible reassurance and beauty, words that are God's reassurance to us of eternal peace — a peace beyond any that our troubled world can know: "He will wipe away every tear from their eyes, and death shall be no more, neither shall there be mourning nor crying nor pain any more, for the former things have passed away" (Apocalypse 21:4).

PART II: SAINT AUGUSTINE'S VISION OF ETERNAL LIFE

The goal of this book has never been to inform anyone of all the theological work that has been done regarding life after death and eternal life, although such work is considerable and of great importance. For those readers who are interested in such a work I strongly suggest *Land of the Living*, written by Monsignor James T. O'Connor, which is an excellent book. There are, of course, a number of popular writers at the present time who have given their own thoughts about this. Many such books are on the market, but it is important to pay attention only to those writers whose ideas are consistent with the teachings of Scripture and Tradition, who think with the mind of the Church. We will continue this pattern of avoiding the overly complex and scholarly as we approach the end of our journey and focus instead on the personal aspects of the search for what really comes next. But now we will do so in the company of one of the great Church Fathers and saints of the Church. We will complete our journey with Saint Augustine.

Obviously, anyone who has ever studied Catholic theology is well aware that Saint Augustine greatly influenced the view of the Church of his time regarding the present subject. It is also true that his influence continues unabated right up to our own day. He returned to the discussion of death and what follows it over and over again. This theme weaves its way through many different pages of his voluminous writings and sermons. It can be found especially in his extensive discussions of the Psalms, in which he frequently addressed the question of what Heaven is going to be like.

This is demonstrated very well in his sermon on Psalm 122 entitled "God Is True Wealth," a good translation of which can be found in its entirety in *Augustine of Hippo: Selected Writings,* part of the Classics of Western Spirituality series. Here Augustine ponders an important question: We know that God is in Heaven and immortal. How is an individual — a human being subject to physical death — given a share in that divine immortality, and how does the individual experience this? Augustine approaches this question with a profound mind and a profound faith. He is able to understand theological ideas in an abstract way and easily sees the limitations of a more literal (or earth-bound) approach. He asks almost scornfully, "Is Heaven our earth above us?" He actually makes fun of the idea that Heaven — eternal life — can be easily equated to anything with which we are familiar. He jokes about it being just up in the sky, saying things like: "Where then are the ladders? For we see so great a distance between earth and heaven, there is such a great separation, such a great space between them. We want to climb there, we see no ladder."[53] Psalm 122 is called a psalm of ascent, meaning that it was originally sung while the priest ascended the Temple steps in Jerusalem. Augustine plays on this fact, asking: "Do we deceive ourselves because we sing the Song of Steps, that is, the Song of Ascent?" He even asks if there are machines that help people get from earth into Heaven.

Saint Augustine makes it more than clear, using quotations from many psalms in addition to Psalm 122, that if we are to grasp it at all we must go beyond the type of literal thinking that imagines Heaven to be a mere physical location, one we imagine to be beyond the sky. He makes a startling statement, showing a profound perception of the nature of our relationship with God. He says that even now in this world, if we have truly united ourselves with Christ, we have already become somewhat united with eternal life, with Heaven. What an astonishing truth this is, and how great it shows the divine love to be. Continuing this theme, Saint Augustine says: "What then is God's heaven?" He answers this question in a way that is startling: "All holy souls, all righteous ones [are Heaven]. The Apostles also, although in the flesh and on earth, were heaven. For the Lord, enthroned in them, traversed the entire world. He then dwells in heaven."[54]

Thus, for Saint Augustine, Heaven is not only a far-off place; it is not only a state of eternal bliss that will be achieved at some distant future time. In its essence, Heaven is a closeness with God; it is God "enthroned" within us. For Saint Augustine, Heaven is always a present possibility and depends on our acceptance of God's love and will deeply into our lives. He explains this by referring to another psalm, Psalm 22. "You dwell in holiness, O praise of Israel" reads the third verse of this psalm, and Saint Augustine uses this to expand his point. "He who dwells in heaven dwells in holiness," he says, seeming to state the obvious.

Then we find Saint Augustine abruptly turning from the psalms to quote Saint Paul. "What is holiness," he asks "but His temple? For 'the temple of God is holy, which temple you are' (1 Corinthians 3:17)." In the surprising and brilliant juxtaposition of these three ideas — that God is by His nature holy; that God's holiness hallows His temple; and that we, the baptized and confirmed, are His temples — Saint Augustine makes plain in only a few words that Heaven (eternal life) is less something to be gained or a place to go than it is someone to know and love. Despite this astounding conclusion, he in no way minimizes the idea that our Heaven will reach its incomparable fullness after this earthly life.

In all this we are reminded of Augustine's famous statement: "Our souls are restless until they rest in You." Here we learn that these words are not simply an excursion into poetics but are a profound theological statement. Our resting in God constitutes eternal Heaven, just as it is God resting in us that enables us to experience some aspects of Heaven during our lives on earth.

These are difficult concepts, and Saint Augustine is aware that the people listening to him have a very rudimentary understanding of eternal life. He understands that he will never be able to dissuade most people from thinking of Heaven as only a physical location. He also understands full well that Heaven, as imagined by most people, is a rather earthly paradise, a worldly city although devoid of sinfulness. This is no less the case today; many people still imagine Heaven to be some kind of wonderful huge happening, sort of like a fair or a great theatrical experience. In reaction to this, Saint Augustine writes in a way that is comprehensible to his readers, and rather than discuss Heaven in any overly abstract way, he uses the metaphor of a city. He states that in this (heavenly) city, unlike in any earthly city, there is true wealth. In fact there can be no wanting in the heavenly city. There we shall have no need of anything but will be satisfied completely. What is this true wealth, of which Saint Augustine speaks? Again it is a metaphor, and again he turns to the words of Saint Paul to explain. It is: "For this perishable nature must put on the imperishable, and this mortal nature must put on immortality. When the perishable puts on the imperishable, and the mortal puts on immortality, then shall come to pass the saying that is written: 'Death is swallowed up in victory' " (1 Corinthians 15:53-54). We should learn, then, that in Saint Augustine's eyes and in Saint Paul's, to achieve this true wealth is to achieve Heaven — the pearl of great price. It is a state of true and perfect righteousness in which we will be incapable not only of doing evil but even of desiring evil.

Saint Augustine develops these thoughts in his monumental work *The City of God*, exploring ideas about eternal life, testing them against Holy Scripture, especially the words of Christ, and attempting to discern more and more of what God has prepared for those who love Him. We will follow Augustine through some passages of *The City of God*, attempting to discern with him what we can.

Saint Augustine takes up the question of the lives of the saints, discussing the state in which they exist beyond the physical world.

He refers to what he calls spiritual and immortal bodies in their flesh. He affirms that they are alive but is careful to say that the lives they live now are not carnal lives as are ours. They live instead in a spiritual way.[55] This is, of course, an extremely mysterious and seemingly contradictory concept. As bodies are by their nature physical, how is it possible to have a body that is spiritual and immortal? Saint Augustine, never one to shy away from a challenge, faces right up to this problem. He writes, "To tell the truth I have no real notion of what eternal life will be like for the simple reason that I have no sensible experience to which it can be related. Nor can I say that I have any mental conception of such an activity for at that height what is intelligence or what can I do? In heaven as Saint Paul assures us 'the peace of God... surpasses all understanding.' "[56]

The Peace of Eternal Life

The next point that Saint Augustine makes in discussing eternal life is that in it we are to be the sharers of God's peace. Although we all understand what peace is, when we try to contemplate the peace of God we once again encounter a concept that stretches our comprehension to its very limit. All human peace is fragile and contingent on a thousand things. The peace of God, however, is imperturbable and indestructible. It is a peace without end. To share in such peace means we are given a supreme degree of peace; it is the measure of our capacity; it is a peace that is unfathomable. Saint Augustine again quotes Saint Paul: "We know in part and we prophesy in part; until that which is perfect is to come.... We see now through a mirror in an obscure way but then face to face" (1 Corinthians 13:9, 12). Clearly that perfect peace lies ahead for us, but as we can participate in Heaven while still on earth by "enthroning" God within us, so we can experience a bit of that peace as well — one we cannot know in full until we see God "face to face."

Augustine then gives us his own meditation, which is quite powerful: "This is how the holy angels are called our angels in the sense that once we have been delivered from the power of darkness we have received the pledge of the spirit and have been translated to the Kingdom of Christ, we shall have begun to belong to the angels, with whom we are to be fellow citizens in that holy and supremely satisfying communion which is the City of God about which I have been writing all these pages."[57]

We can readily see the importance that Saint Augustine assigns to the angels. In his view these spiritual beings will, along with all the saved, be the inhabitants of Heaven. It is they who first experienced and continue to experience that which is our goal: to be face-to-face with God. In present Catholic life, by contrast, there seems to be very little consideration of the angels and even less of the guardian angels. However, they are spoken of by Christ, and this is something that we should never overlook. Augustine is very clear that Christ speaks of our own angels. Speaking of children, Christ warns, "See that you do not despise one of these little ones; for I tell you that in heaven their angels always behold the face of my Father who is in heaven" (Matthew 18:10), showing once again that the betrayal or mistreatment of the innocent is a sin of great proportions.

Seeing God Face-to-Face

Augustine spends a good deal of time pondering what it means to "see God face-to-face." Clearly this is a concept of great importance to him as he meditates on the nature of eternal life. This seeing of God "face-to-face" represents for him the fullness of eternal life, the completion of all that is implied when he earlier claimed that Heaven begins when God is "enthroned" within us. But of what does this mysterious type of seeing consist? It is not entirely a metaphor for Augustine — although surely there are strong metaphorical aspects to it — because he is careful to discuss whether or not it will be accomplished through physical or spiritual eyes. Augustine, as always, finds the perfect scriptural reference to support his thought. He speaks of Jesus's Sermon on the Mount, another place in which "seeing" is all important. "Blessed are the pure in heart for they shall see God" (Matthew 5:8), Augustine quotes, showing us that whatever type of seeing is involved, our vision of the divine can be easily obscured by sin. He then writes, "No Christian reading these words in a spirit of faith has any doubt that when God is to be seen, he will be seen with the eyes of the heart, but of course the problem I am now dealing with is whether in heaven God will also be seen with the eyes of the body."[58]

Saint Augustine ponders further the concept of seeing God, finding in it a way to better comprehend eternal life. He concentrates on the words of Saint Paul that suggest that we are face-to-face with God (1 Corinthians 13:12), raising once again the question of whether it is possible to see God with our material eyes. Saint Paul shows that we are really made to see God, but that it is our many sins that prevent this from happening through the darkening of the intellect and the confusing of our wills. Our seeing God will be the overwhelming encounter that transforms our mortal lives into eternal lives. Otherwise Saint Paul would not have written, "And we all, with unveiled face, beholding the glory of the Lord, are being changed into his likeness from one degree of glory to another; for this comes from the Lord who is the Spirit." (2 Corinthians 3:18). Augustine, whose powerful mind is able to see all aspects of a question, ponders the sight of God from every possible angle and finds in it much that increases his faith in eternal life. He does, however, end his discussion with the admission that full understanding has not been gained and is not even possible. He admits that the eternal life of which he is certain is a slowly unfolding mystery to those whose sojourns on earth have not yet ended. To illustrate this he quotes words from the Book of Wisdom, saying, "for the reasoning of mortals is worthless, and our designs are likely to fail" (Wisdom 9:14).

After a long, philosophical discussion during which Saint Augustine disagrees with a popular philosophy of the time, he comes to this conclusion about the seeing of God:

> What... is possible and highly probable is that we shall be able to see the material bodies of the new heaven and the new earth in such a way that by means of our own bodies and of all the others which we shall see wherever our eyes are turned, we shall see God, and we shall see Him with utmost clarity as being everywhere present and as regulating

the whole universe, including material things. We shall see Him in a way different from the ways in which His "invisible attributes" are now seen, "being understood by the things that are made," for "we see now through a mirror in an obscure manner" and only "in part," and we must rely more on the eyes of faith, whereby we believe, than on the eyes of the body, whereby we see the beauty of the material world.[59]

Here Saint Augustine tells us that in Heaven our physical eyes will still see physical objects such as trees. However, in seeing a tree we will see not only its physical nature, but with perfect clarity we will perceive why the tree is there and how it fits harmoniously into the whole of creation, which brings us face-to-face with God. With the clarified vision of Heaven, we will see the tree as an expression of the eternal creative presence of God.

Finally, Saint Augustine reminds us of the warning of Saint Paul, who wrote: "Therefore do not pronounce judgment before the time, before the Lord comes, who will bring to light the things now hidden in darkness and will disclose the purposes of the heart. Then every man will receive his commendation from God" (1 Corinthians 4:5). We may prayerfully speculate on the "commendation from God" — that is, the rewards that He has in store for us in eternal life. But it is only Christ who will reveal the truth, and that will come in God's own time.

At the end of this discussion Saint Augustine finally offers two hypotheses in regards to our seeing God. The first is that we see God with our own eyes, which are configured to resemble the powers of the mind, "to enable them to perceive what is by nature immaterial."[60] In this hypothesis, which seems improbable to Saint Augustine, the natural ability of the eye is somehow mysteriously elevated. The second hypothesis is that we perceive God in many ways. "He will be seen in the spirit (whereby each of us will see Him in ourselves and in one another); He will be seen in Himself; He will be seen in the new Heaven and the new earth and in every creature then existing: and by means of our bodies He will be seen in every material object towards which the eyes of our spiritual bodies happen to direct their gaze."[61] One way or another he sets up the idea that we do, in fact, see God, and in this seeing we encounter Heaven. "Wherever we shall turn the eyes of our spiritual bodies we shall see the immaterial God, ruling all things, and we shall see him by means of our bodies."[62]

Of What Does the Happiness of Heaven Consist?

Saint Augustine now takes up the question of the personal experience of Heaven. For him Heaven is a happiness that no evil can touch. It is a life that consists of endless and joyful praising of God. This involves no weariness, no trace of toil, no waste of energy, but only praise: "Every fiber and organ of our imperishable body will play its part in the praising of God. On earth these varied organs have each a special function, but, in heaven these functions are swallowed up in felicity in the perfect certainty of an untroubled everlastingness of joy."[63] He speaks of God as the supreme artist who has fashioned us both within and without in every fiber of our being.

When we think about our bodies in eternal life, we realize we have come to a very mysterious question. Augustine says, "There will be such poise, such grace, such beauty as become a place where nothing unbecoming can be found. Wherever the spirit wills, there in a flash, will the body be. Nor will the spirit ever will anything unbecoming either to itself or to the body."[64] As "seeing God" presented problems to "our frail and feeble minds," so the concept of a body participating in the eternal life that we call Heaven presents problems, as well. In Augustine's concept, the body, while remaining a body, seems incorporeal. Distance is nothing to it, barriers do not impede it. Augustine sees in these bodies which enjoy eternal life a perfect joining of matter to spirit; thought and action become one. They are like the body of the Risen Christ, who walks through walls to meet the Apostles in the Cenacle. These bodies are the same as they always were, yet profoundly different. They are perfected in ways we can only begin to imagine.

Augustine makes it very clear that happiness is part of eternal life. He makes it equally clear that such happiness has but one source: It is founded entirely on God Himself. "God will be the source of every satisfaction more than any heart can rightly crave, more than life and health, food and wealth, glory and honor, peace and every good — so that God, as Saint Paul said, 'may be all in all.' "[65] Saint Augustine continues his meditation on eternal life, growing more and more excited, his words becoming more and more a rhapsody until finally he says, "And in this great gift of vision this response of love this paean of praise all alike will share as all will share in everlasting life."[66] He then speaks of the great ranks upon ranks of the saints whom he mentions are graded according to their merit and honor. Despite this "there will be no envy of the lower for the higher, as there is no envy of the angel for the archangel — for this is one of the great blessednesses of the blessed City. The less rewarded will be linked in perfect peace with the more highly favored...."[67]

One of the great gifts of our heavenly Father is freedom of will. Alone of all material creation humankind possesses this. Does it continue into eternal life? If so, how would it be exercised? Without it we feel ourselves less than we were created to be, yet can we hope that such freedom persists into eternal life? We cannot imagine ourselves without it. Saint Augustine, a man whose will was powerful, does not neglect this question. He sees how important this gift is to the human soul and states that it must remain. In a mysterious way, he claims, there is freedom to choose good or evil even in Heaven, but because in Heaven one is always turned to God, no sin could possibly be desired — in the Beatific Vision, all desires have been satisfied. In experiencing the love of God, one could have no desire for sin, no yearning to turn from perfection to that which is less. We are given more, not less, freedom in eternal life: the freedom to love perfectly, which is the freedom not to sin; and the last freedom, the freedom from the power to sin. Augustine realizes the importance of this question and writes:

> Our will will be ineradicably rooted in rectitude and love as in beatitude. It is true that with Adam's sin we lost our right to grace and glory, but with our right, we did not lose our longing to be happy. And as for freedom, can we think that

God Himself, who certainly cannot sin is therefore without freedom? The conclusion is that, in the Everlasting City there will remain in each and all of us an inalienable freedom of the will emancipating us from every evil and filling us with every good. Rejoicing in the inexhaustible beatitude of everlasting happiness unclouded by the memory of any sin or sanction suffered, yet with no forgetfulness of our redemption nor any gratitude for our redeemer.[68]

Here Augustine deals with an important problem, the recollection of our past misdeeds and miseries in Heaven. Many have wondered if they somehow continue to haunt us or if forgetfulness prevents us from regretting our many sins? Perhaps we live in eternal life with full awareness of our many shortcomings yet without feelings. Saint Augustine is concerned about this as well, and he compares our remembrance of our sinfulness with the pain that it causes us. This is done with the thoughts of a philosopher who contemplates such deeds in the abstract. Saint Augustine claims that our sins, forgiven by God and put behind us, will cause us no more remorse. He claims that those deeds will belong to us no longer in the way the deeds that the philosopher contemplates do not belong to him. Saint Augustine even goes so far as to say that a man studying medicine does not suffer the pains and symptoms that he has studied.

Finally, Saint Augustine very much equates eternal life to the eternal rest or the Sabbath of God. He compares the seventh day of Creation to the seventh day of the week, the day that is a divinely mandated day of rest for the Jewish people. A man who was well acquainted with physical suffering and labor, with backbreaking work in the fields, with the intense labor that characterized his society, Augustine wrote about the difficulties and unending weariness of those people who faced such labor every day of their lives. As a minor aristocrat, he was not among such laborers, but he was very sensitive to the notion of Sabbath, far more sensitive than we who have never known such labor.

"Six days shall work be done, but the seventh day is a Sabbath of solemn rest, holy to the LORD.... Therefore the people of Israel shall keep the Sabbath, observing the Sabbath throughout their generations, as a perpetual covenant. It is a sign for ever between me and the people of Israel that in six days the Lord made heaven and earth, and on the seventh day he rested, and was refreshed," says the Book of Exodus (31:15, 16-17), linking Sabbath rest both to God's covenant and to creation and making such rest an imitation of the divine. Augustine writes of eternal life as Sabbath — a Sabbath marked by joy and without end: "This, indeed, will be the ultimate Sabbath that has no evening which the Lord foreshadowed in the account of His creation...."[69] Augustine continues to write, "... we ourselves will be a 'seventh day' when we shall be filled with his blessing and remade by his sanctification. In the stillness of that rest we shall see that he is the God of divinity we ambitioned for ourselves when we listened to the seducer's words, 'You shall be as Gods,' and so fell away from Him, the true God who would have given us a divinity of participation that could never be gained by desertion."[70]

In those beautiful lines, Saint Augustine tells us that in eternal life we shall not only participate in Sabbath rest but actually "become" Sabbath rest. The peace and wholeness of Heaven will so pervade our beings that we will be sanctified and made able to partake in the divine serenity. In that serenity, shared with God, we will know our heavenly Father in a new and more profound way. His peace will hallow us, transforming us into beings of peace and tranquility — beings who experience the eternal bliss of Sabbath. We will understand that all that we sought during our lives on earth has been realized in the vision we now have of God; we will know that all our earthly wantings were really for God, that He alone was all that we ever needed. At last we will be satiated; at last we will be at peace.

Very near the conclusion of his great work, *The City of God*, Saint Augustine writes these words: "Suffice it to say that this 'seventh day' will be our Sabbath and that it will end in no evening but only in the Lord's Day — that eighth and eternal day which dawned when Christ's resurrection heralded an eternal rest both for the spirit and the body. On that day we shall rest and see, see and love and praise — for this is to be the end without the end of all our living, that Kingdom without end, the real goal of our present life."[71]

As we have meditated on these words of Saint Augustine, which are filled with the insights of Scripture and the traditions of the Church, our minds have been opened to some of the mysteries and particularly some of the glorious beauty of eternal life. We cannot, however, fully understand — much less completely appreciate — everlasting life. It should, however, fill us with great awe and wonder, with profound gratitude to the Father who offers His own eternity to us, to the Son whose coming among us a man and dying for us makes eternal life possible for us, to the Holy Spirit who works to bring us to eternal life constantly.

AFTERWORD

"Into paradise may the angels lead you. At
your coming may the martyrs receive you, and
bring you into the holy city, Jerusalem."

IN PARADISUM[72]

Our journey beyond the cosmos has ended. We have met
"Sister Bodily Death"; we have glimpsed the realities of
judgment and purgation, of eternal loss and eternal bliss. But we
have only glimpsed them; for, as I have said so many times already,
their realities exceed what our "frail and feeble minds" are capable
of fully understanding. However, God, whose love for us is im-
measurable, does allow us some comprehension. That little bit of
knowledge should bring us joy and renewed faith. It should help
us to face the difficulties that attend all human lives; it should help
us to remember that, as Saint Augustine has so wisely shown us,
the beginning of our Heaven can be experienced even now. As
we strive to imitate Jesus, to love others fully, to "enthrone God
within us," we meet the source of all things, the God who is love
and who yearns to give us eternal life.

If we love others, we must show that love by being concerned
about those who might be in danger of losing their souls, for
we have seen that the possibility of Hell exists for us all. If you
read the lives of the saints, you will see that many of them spent
significant parts of their lives praying for the salvation of others
and working in any way that they could by preaching, apostolic
teaching, and good works ranging from education to the care of
the sick and dying. Few of us are great saints, but each of us can
do our part.

It is an unfortunate fact as we look at our present situation in
the United States and the Western nations that there appears to

be less and less interest in the salvation of others or perhaps even in struggling to fulfill the needs of one's own salvation. When I was in high school, I was very aware of clergy, sisters, and laity around me who were working toward salvation for themselves and other people. That interest seems to be lost in many ways. We do understand that human weakness explains much misbehavior or at least indifference, but we have become so accepting that we are indulgent. I hope that those who have read this book will take very seriously the meaning of their salvation and that of others and strive to follow the teachings of Christ, remembering always that if we love Him, we must keep His commandments. If we do so, bodily death will truly become our gentle sister, and we will be able to face her at the end of life as did my good and saintly friend Terence Cardinal Cooke, who wrote only days before his death, "I have absolute faith in the message of our Lord and Savior Jesus Christ. I believe that he has indeed gone to prepare a place for us and that He calls us to eternal life and peace."

ONE FINAL NOTE

"But What About the Cat?"

A great many people have found much company, joy, and even love from a pet. As a result, every sympathetic priest has heard the following question more times than he can count: "What about my cat . . . or dog . . . or horse . . . or hamster after death?" No one can answer this question for sure, but we can engage in some reasonable speculation.

Quite a number of theological writers have expressed the hope that at least some members of the animal world will also be part of the heavenly world. Saint Augustine points out that all the ecology we know in our earthly lives will also be represented in Heaven, although we must admit that this is not the view of some other writers.

It would seem to me that although animals can have no right to eternal life — as even human beings only receive this by grace — is it not reasonable to hope that an animal who has helped us along our way through life, and had a real share of our affections, may also be with us (recreated, so to speak) in our heavenly home? Some will laugh. Some will ridicule. But many will at least hope that they will find their animal friends, who have meant so much in this life, with them in the next. At least we can state with confidence that no one can say it is absolutely impossible. Pope John Paul II spoke of animals and their value in God's eyes in a public audience in 1990. He never said they would be in Heaven, but he did say that "the animals also have a vital breath . . . and that they received it from God. Under this aspect man, coming forth from the hands of God, *appears in solidarity with all living beings.*"[73]

That's more than enough to give us hope.

Prayers, Poems, and Meditations

The following quotations have been culled from various sources. I hope they will be of some aid to you as you pray and meditate on the end of bodily life, judgment, and the glorious hope that follows it. I have included writers of different points of view, but all of them share with us the fervent belief in God's bright promise of eternal life. You will notice that no quotations from the Gospels appear among those drawn from Holy Scripture. This is certainly not because they are unimportant but only because such quotations were presented in large numbers in the previous chapters.

From the Old Testament

For everything there is a season, and a time for every matter under heaven:

> a time to be born, and a time to die;
> a time to plant, and a time to pluck up what is planted;
> a time to kill, and a time to heal;
> a time to break down, and a time to build up;
> a time to weep, and a time to laugh;
> a time to mourn, and a time to dance;
> a time to cast away stones, and a time to gather
>   stones together;
> a time to embrace, and a time to refrain from
>   embracing;
> a time to seek, and a time to lose;
> a time to keep, and a time to cast away;
> a time to rend, and a time to sew;
> a time to keep silence, and a time to speak;
> a time to love, and a time to hate;
> a time for war, and a time for peace.

ECCLESIASTES 3:1–8

But the souls of the righteous are in the hand of God,
    and no torment will ever touch them.
In the eyes of the foolish they seemed to have died, and
    their departure was thought to be an affliction,
and their going from us to be their destruction; but they
    are at peace.
    For though in the sight of men they were punished,
        their hope is full of immortality.

WISDOM 3:1–4

... he will destroy on this mountain the covering that is cast over all peoples, the veil that is spread over all nations. He will swallow up death for ever, and the Lord GOD will wipe away tears from all faces, and the reproach of his people he will take away from all the earth....

ISAIAH 25:7–8

The Spirit of the Lord GOD is upon me,
    because the LORD has anointed me
to bring good tidings to the afflicted;
    he has sent me to bind up the brokenhearted,
to proclaim liberty to the captives,
      and the opening of the prison to those who are
        bound;
to proclaim the year of the LORD's favor,
    and the day of vengeance of our God;
    to comfort all who mourn;
to grant to those who mourn in Zion —
    to give them a garland instead of ashes,
the oil of gladness instead of mourning,
    the mantle of praise instead of a faint spirit;
that they may be called oaks of righteousness,
the planting of the LORD, that he may be glorified.

ISAIAH 61:1–3

I will extol thee, O LORD, for thou hast drawn me up,
    and hast not let my foes rejoice over me.
O LORD my God, I cried to thee for help,
    and thou hast healed me.
O LORD, thou hast brought up my soul from Sheol,
    restored me to life from among those gone down to
        the Pit.

PSALM 30:1-3

For I know that my Redeemer lives,
    and at last he will stand upon the earth;
and after my skin has been thus destroyed,
    then from my flesh I shall see God,
whom I shall see on my side,
    and my eyes shall behold, and not another.

JOB 19:25-27

From the New Testament

Do you not know that all of us who have been baptized into Christ Jesus were baptized into his death? We were buried therefore with him by baptism into death, so that as Christ was raised from the dead by the glory of the Father, we too might walk in newness of life.

For if we have been united with him in a death like his, we shall certainly be united with him in a resurrection like his. We know that our old self was crucified with him so that the sinful body might be destroyed, and we might no longer be enslaved to sin. For he who has died is freed from sin. But if we have died with Christ, we believe that we shall also live with him. For we know that Christ being raised from the dead will never die again; death no longer has dominion over him. The death he died he died to sin, once for all, but the life he lives he lives to God. So you also must consider yourselves dead to sin and alive to God in Christ Jesus.

ROMANS 6:3-11

So we do not lose heart. Though our outer nature is wasting away, our inner nature is being renewed every day. For this slight momentary affliction is preparing for us an eternal weight of glory beyond all comparison, because we look not to the things that are seen but to the things that are unseen; for the things that are seen are transient, but the things that are unseen are eternal.

2 CORINTHIANS 4:16-18

... our commonwealth is in heaven, and from it we await a Savior, the Lord Jesus Christ, who will change our lowly body to be like his glorious body, by the power which enables him even to subject all things to himself.

PHILIPPIANS 3:20-21

Blessed be the God and Father of our Lord Jesus Christ! By his great mercy we have been born anew to a living hope through the resurrection of Jesus Christ from the dead, and to an inheritance which is imperishable, undefiled, and unfading, kept in heaven for you, who by God's power are guarded through faith for a salvation ready to be revealed in the last time. In this you rejoice, though now for a little while you may have to suffer various trials, so that the genuineness of your faith, more precious than gold which though perishable is tested by fire, may redound to praise and glory and honor at the revelation of Jesus Christ. Without having seen him you love him; though you do not now see him you believe in him and rejoice with unutterable and exalted joy. As the outcome of your faith you obtain the salvation of your souls.

1 PETER 1:3-9

From Poetry

The Canticle of the Sun
Most High, All Powerful, God of Goodness;
To Thee be praise and glory,

Honour and all thankfulness
To Thee alone, Most High, are these things due,
And no man is worthy to speak of Thee.

Be Thou praised, O Lord, for all Thy creation,
More especially for our Brother the Sun,
Who bringeth forth the day and givest light thereby,
For he is glorious and splendid in his radiance,
And to Thee, Most High, he bears similitude.

Be Thou praised, O Lord, for our Sister the Moon,
And for the Stars in the heavens,
Thou has set them bright and sparkling and beautiful.

Be Thou praised, O Lord, for our Brother the Wind,
For the air and for the clouds,
For serene and tempestuous days,
For through these dost Thou sustain all living things.

Be Thou Praised, O Lord, for our Sister the Water,
For she giveth boundless service,
And is lowly, precious and pure.

Be Thou praised, O Lord, for our Brother the Fire,
Through whom Thou givest light in the night hours,
For he is beautiful and joyous, vigorous and strong.

Be Thou praised, O Lord, for our Sister Mother Earth,
Who doth nourish us and ruleth over us,
And bringeth forth divers fruits,
And bright flowers and herbs.

Be Thou praised, O Lord,
For those who show forgiveness through Thy love,
And that do endure sickness and sorrow,
Blessed are they that do suffer in lowliness of spirit,
For by Thee, Most High, shall they be exalted.

Be Thou praised, O Lord, for our Sister Bodily Death,
From whom no man living may escape.
Woe to those who die in mortal sin.

Blessed are they who shall be found doing Thy most
    Holy Will,
For the second dying shall work them no evil.

Be Thou praised and blessed, O Lord,
In endless thanksgiving,
And served in all humility.

SAINT FRANCIS OF ASSISI
The Hymn of the Sun, p. 9

Death Be Not Proud

Death be not proud, though some have called thee
Mighty and dreadful, for thou art not so;
For those who thou think'st thou doest overthrow
Die not, poor Death, nor yet canst thou kill me.
From rest and sleep, which but thy pictures be,
Much pleasure; then from thee much more must flow,
And soonest our best men with thee do go.
Rest of their bones, and soul's delivery.
Thou are slave to fate, chance, kings, and desperate
    men,
And dost with poison, war, and sickness dwell;
And poppy or charms can make us sleep as well
And better than they stroke; why swell'st thou then?
One short sleep past, we wake eternally,
And death shall be no more: Death, thou shalt die.

JOHN DONNE
The Norton Anthology of English Literature,
Vol. I, p. 909

The Dying Christian to His Soul

Vital spark of heav'nly flame,
Quit, oh, quit, this mortal frame!
Trembling, hoping, ling'ring, flying,
Oh, the pain, the bliss of dying!

Cease, fond Nature, cease thy strife,
And let me languish into life!

Hark! they whisper; Angels say,
Sister Spirit, come away.
What is this absorbs me quite,
Steals my senses, shuts my sight,
Drowns my spirits, draws my breath?
Tell me, my Soul! can this be Death?

The world recedes; it disappears;
Heav'n opens on my eyes; my ears
With sounds seraphic ring:
Lend, lend your wings! I mount! I fly!
O Grave! where is thy Victory?
O Death! where is thy Sting?

ALEXANDER POPE
The Oxford Book of English Verse,
no. 453

Death

Death, thou wast once an uncouth hideous thing,
Nothing but bones,
The sad effect of sadder groans:
Thy mouth was open, but thou couldst not sing.

For we considered thee as at some six
Or ten years hence,
After the loss of life and sense,
Flesh being turned to dust, and bones to sticks.

We looked on this side of thee, shooting short;
Where we did find
The shells of fledge souls left behind,
Dry dust, which sheds no tears, but may extort.

But since our Savior's death did put some blood
Into thy face,

Thou art grown fair and full of grace,
Much in request, much sought for as a good.

For we do now behold thee gay and glad,
As at Doomsday;
When souls shall wear their new array,
And all thy bones with beauty shall be clad.

Therefore we can go die as sleep, and trust
Half that we have
Unto an honest faithful grave;
Making our pillows either down, or dust.

George Herbert
The Norton Anthology of Poetry, p. 267

Death Is a Dialogue

Death is a dialogue between
The spirit and the dust.
"Dissolve," says Death — The Spirit, "Sir,"
I have another trust" —

Death doubts it — Argues from the Ground —
The Spirit turns away,
Just laying off for evidence,
An overcoat of clay.

Emily Dickenson
The Complete Poems of Emily Dickinson,
no. 976

When Earth's Last Picture Is Painted

When Earth's last picture is painted, and the tubes are
    twisted and dried,
When the oldest colors have faded, and the youngest
    critic has died,
We shall rest, and, faith, we shall need it — lie down for
    an aeon or two,

Till the Master of All Good Workmen shall set us to
work anew!

And those that were good shall be happy: they shall sit
in a golden chair;
They shall splash at a ten-league canvas with brushes of
comets' hair;
They shall find real saints to draw from — Magdalene,
Peter, and Paul,
They shall work for an age at a sitting and never be tired
at all!

And only the Master shall praise us, and only the Master
shall blame;
And no one shall work for money, and no one shall
work for fame;
But each for the joy of the working, and each, in his
separate star;
Shall draw the Thing as he sees it, for the God of
Things as They Are!

RUDYARD KIPLING
Rudyard Kipling's Verse, p. 226

Consolation

When I sink down in gloom or fear.
Hope blighted or delay'd
Thy whisper, Lord, my heart shall cheer
" 'Tis I; be not afraid!"

Or, startled at some sudden blow
If fretful thought I feel.
"Fear not, it is but I" shall flow
As balm my wound to heal.

Nor will I quit Thy way, though foes
Some onward pass defend;
From each rough voice the watchword goes
"Be not afraid!... a friend!"

And oh! When judgment's trumpet clear
Awakes me from the grave
Still in its echo may I hear
" 'Tis Christ: He comes to save."

CARDINAL JOHN HENRY NEWMAN
Prayers, Verses, and Devotions, p. 591

"If I Were Dead"

If I were dead, you'd sometimes say,
Poor Child!'
The dear lips quiver'd as they spake,
And the tears brake
From eyes which, not to grieve me, brightly smiled.
Poor Child, poor Child!
I seem to hear your laugh, your talk, your song.
It is not true that Love will do no wrong.
Poor Child!
And did you think, when you so cried and smiled,
How I, in lonely nights, should lie awake,
And of those words your full avengers make?
Poor Child, poor Child!
And now, unless it be
That sweet amends thrice told are come to thee,
O God, have Thou no mercy upon me!
Poor Child!

COVENTRY PATMORE
The World's Great Catholic Poetry, p. 264

The Hope of the Resurrection

Though I have watched so many mourners weep
O'er the real dead, in dull earth laid asleep —
Those dead seemed but the shadows of my days
That passed and left me in the sun's bright rays.
Now though you go on smiling in the sun

Our love is slain, and love and you were one.
You are the first, you I have known so long,
Whose death was deadly, a tremendous wrong.
Therefore I seek the faith that sets it right
Amid the lilies and the candle-light.
I think on Heaven, for in that air so dear
We two may meet, confused and parted here.
Ah, when man's dearest dies, 'tis then he goes
To that old balm that heals the centuries' woes.
Then Christ's wild cry in all the streets is rife: —
"I am the Resurrection and the Life."

VACHEL LINDSAY
Collected Poems of Vachel Lindsay, p. 278

From Various Prose Sources

For this reason did Christ die and rise again: to be Lord over death and life. For God indeed is God not of dead bodies, but rather of living persons.

So when the dead arise to life after having been freed from corruption, they will no longer be mortal — these future participants in Christ's resurrection. For no other reason did Christ descend to earth with its metal barriers that block eternity but to crack those bronze doors and smash their iron bars and thereby lead us away from corruption to himself and make us free instead of slaves. Even though this aspect of the divine economy may not yet be realized — since men still die and their bodies decay and are buried — do not lose faith. For at the present time, long before the wondrous things just mentioned will happen, we already have received a pledge in the form of first fruits; and by this pledge we attain to heaven's heights and are seated alongside him who takes us to himself. Somewhere Paul put it this way: "He has raised us along with himself, and he has made us sit in his company on heavenly thrones." We shall enjoy that blessed eventuality in full when the time eternally decreed by the Father shall have arrived, when we lay aside our immaturity and come to perfect manhood.

SAINT ANASTASIUS OF ANTIOCH
From a homily on the Resurrection of Christ
found in the Office for the Dead,
The Monastic Diurnal Revised, p. 632

A strange thing happens to the man who really loves, for even before his own death his life becomes a life with the dead. Could a true lover ever forget his dead? When one has really loved, his forgetting is only apparent, he only *seems* to get over his grief. The quiet and composure he gradually regains are not a sign that things are as they were before, but a proof that his grief is ultimate and definitive. It shows that a piece of his own heart has really died and is now with the living dead. This is the real reason he can weep no more.

Thus I am living now with the dead, with those who have gone before me into the dark night of death, where no man can work. But how can I really live with the dead? How can I continue to find life in the one bond left between us, the bond of our mutual love? Deign to answer me, O God, for you have called Yourself the God of the living and not of the dead.

... I live more and more with those who have gone before me into the dark night where no man can work. By Your life-giving graces, O lord, let it become ever more a life of faith in Your life, shining now dimly in this earthly night. Let me live with the living who have preceded me in the sign of faith, who have gone before me into the bright day of eternal life when no man need work, because You Yourself are this day, the Fullness of all Reality, the God of the Living.

When I pray, "Grant them eternal rest, O Lord, and let Thy perpetual light shine upon them," let my words be only the echo of the prayer of love that they themselves are speaking for me in the silence of eternity: "O Lord, grant unto him, whom we love in Your Love now as never before, grant unto him after his life's struggle Your eternal rest, and let Your perpetual light shine upon him, as it does on us."

KARL RAHNER
Prayers for a Lifetime, pp. 145, 148-149

Our existence carries eternity within itself. "He planted life eternal within us." Because we can do the eternal at any moment, the will of God, dying too is doing the will of God. Just as being is obedience to the Creator, so dying is returning to the Source.

Death may be a supreme spiritual act, turning oneself over to eternity. The moment of death, a moment of ecstasy. A moment of no return to vanity.

Thus afterlife is felt to be a reunion and all of life a preparation for it....

Death may be the beginning of the exaltation, an ultimate celebration, a reunion of the divine image with the divine source of being.

Dust returns to dust, while the image, the divine stake in man, is restored to the bundle of life.

Death is not sensed as a defeat but as a summation, an arrival, a conclusion.

"O God, the soul whom Thou hast placed within me is pure. Thou hast created it Thou hast formed it; Thou hast breathed it into me. Thou preservest it within me; Thou will take it from me and restore it to me in the hereafter. So long as the soul is within me, I offer thanks before thee... Lord of all souls. Blessed are Thou, O Lord, who restorest the souls to the dead."

The meaning of death is in return.

ABRAHAM JOSHUA HESCHEL
"Death Is a Homecoming,"
from *Moral Grandeur and Spiritual Audacity*, p. 371

We give back to you, O God, those whom you gave to us. You did not lose them when you gave them to us, and we do not lose them by their return to you. Your dear Son has taught us that life is eternal and love cannot die. So death is only an horizon, and an horizon is only the limit of our sight. Open our eyes to see more clearly, and draw us closer to you that we may know that we are nearer to our loved ones, who are with you. You have told us that you are pre-paring a place for us: prepare for us also for that happy place, that where you are we may also be always, O dear Lord of life and death.

WILLIAM PENN
The Oxford Book of Prayer, no. 541

[W]e are called to live a particular communication with our deceased. In faith and prayer, we re-establish our fam-ily links with them; they watch us, follow after us and assist us. They already see the Lord just "as he is." So they en-courage us to continue on the way, that pilgrimage which still remains to us on earth. The fact is that we "have no lasting city" here (Hebrews 13:14). The important thing is for us not to grow weary, above all not to lose sight of the ultimate goal. Our departed are there where we too shall be. Indeed there is common ground between us and them, which makes us neighbors. It is the ground of our mutual introduction into the trinitarian mystery of Father, Son, and Holy Spirit, on the basis of the same baptism. We here touch hands, because death does not exist on this ground; there is but a single flow of unending life.

POPE JOHN PAUL II
Prayers and Devotions, p. 380

We are strangers before Thee, O God, and sojourners as were our fathers; our days on earth vanish like shadows. But the speedy flight of life, and the gloom of the grave should not dismay us, but should teach us wisdom. It should prompt us to put our trust in Thee, who wilt not suffer Thy children to see destruction. For the dust returns to the dust; the spirit which Thou hast breathed into us returns to Thee, its ever-living source. Into us Thou has infused a portion of Thy divinity; within us we sense our own weakness and Thy mighty strength. Human achievements are transitory and human strivings vain; but Thy word endureth forever, and Thy purposes are fulfilled. When we become servants of Thy Law, witnesses of Thy truth, champions of Thy kingdom, then indeed do we endow our fleeting days with abiding value.

O that we might die the death of the righteous and our end be like theirs. Suffer us not to pass away in our sins, O Judge of life and death. Teach us so to number our days, that we may get us a heart of wisdom. Grant us strength and understanding, that we may not delay to remove from our midst all that is displeasing in Thy sight, and thus become reconciled with Thee.

The Union Prayerbook II, pp. 310–311

Heaven cannot be pictured in our imagination,
For we can imagine only what we can see —
The things of this earth.
Since heaven is so different, we sometimes wonder,
Will we not feel out of place there,
A bit strange and uneasy?
We shall not feel out of place,
Strange and uneasy
For we are home:
Home with God our Father and His Spirit,
Home with Christ our Lord,
Home with Mary our mother,
Home with the saints, the cherished ones of God.
And we are happy:
Eye has not seen
Nor ear heard
Nor has it entered into the heart of man
What things God has prepared
For those who love Him.
Like the men of the gospel parable
We count no sacrifice too great to purchase the field

In which lies the hidden treasure.
With Saint Paul
We reckon that the sufferings of the present time
Are not worthy to be compared with the glory to come
That will be revealed to us.

Challenge, a Jesuit prayer book, p. 230

All God's providences, all God's dealings with us, all His judgments, mercies, warning, deliverance, tend to peace and repose as their ultimate issue. All our troubles and pleasure here, all our anxieties, fears, doubts, difficulties, hopes, encouragements, afflictions, losses, attainments, tend this one way. After Christmas, Easter, Whitsuntide, comes Trinity Sunday, and the weeks that follow; and in like manner, after our soul's anxious travail; after the birth of the Spirit; after trial and temptation; after sorrow and pain; after daily dyings to the world; after daily risings unto holiness; at length comes that "rest which remaineth unto the people of God". After the fever of life; after weariness and sicknesses' fightings and despondings; languor and fretfulness; struggling and failing; struggling and succeeding; after all the changes and chances of this troubled unhealthy state, at length comes death, at length the White Throne of God, at length the Beatific Vision.

CARDINAL JOHN HENRY NEWMAN
The Heart of Newman, p. 254

He sought his former accustomed fear of death and did not find it. "Where is it? What death?" There was no fear because there was no death.

In place of death there was light.

"So that's what it is!" he suddenly exclaimed aloud. "What joy!"

To him all this happened in single instant, and the meaning of that instant did not change. For those present his agony continued for another two hours. Something rattled in his throat, his emaciated body twitched, then the gasping and rattle became less and less frequent.

"It is finished!" said someone near him.

He heard these words and repeated them in his soul.

"Death is finished." He said to himself. "It is no more!"

He drew in a breath, stopped in the midst of a sigh, stretched out and died.

LEO TOLSTOY
"The Death of Ivan Ilych,"
from *Great Short Works of Leo Tolstoy*, p. 302

I wait, O God, with patience and in hope. I wait like a blind man who has been promised the dawning of light. I await the resurrection of the dead and of the flesh.

KARL RAHNER
Prayers for a Lifetime, p. 161

Prayers

Prayer for a Happy Death

O God, great and omnipotent judge of the living and the dead, we are to appear before you after this short life to render an account of our works. Give us the grace to prepare for our last hour by a devout and holy life, and protect us against a sudden and unprovided death. Let us remember our frailty and mortality, that we may always live in the ways of your commandments. Teach us to "watch and pray" (Luke 21:36), that when your summons comes for our departure from this world, we may go forth to meet you, experience a merciful judgment, and rejoice in everlasting happiness. We ask this through Christ our Lord. Amen.

Prayer to Mary for a Happy Death

O Mary, conceived without sin, pray for us who have recourse to you. O Refuge of Sinners, Mother of the dying, forsake us not at the hour of our death. Obtain for us the grace of perfect sorrow, sincere contrition, the pardon and remission of our sins, a worthy receiving of the holy Viaticum and the comfort of the sacrament of Extreme Unction, in order that we may appear with greater security before the throne of the just but merciful judge, our God and our Redeemer.

A Prayer for the Dead

God our Father,
Your power brings us to birth,
Your providence guides our lives,
and by Your command we return to dust.

Lord, those who die still live in Your presence,
their lives change but do not end.
I pray in hope for my family,
relatives and friends,
and for all the dead known to You alone.

In company with Christ,
Who died and now lives,
may they rejoice in Your kingdom,
where all our tears are wiped away.
Unite us together again in one family,
to sing Your praise forever and ever. Amen.

A Prayer for the Dying and a Special Soul

O most merciful Jesus,
Lover of souls,
I beseech Thee,
by the agony of Thy most Sacred Heart,
and by the sorrows of Thine Immaculate Mother,
wash clean in Thy Blood
the sinners of the whole world
who are to die this day.

Remember most especially the soul I spiritually adopt
with the intention of entrusting him or her to Thy
Shepherd's care:
I beseech Thee for the grace to move this sinner,
who is in danger of going to Hell, to repent.
I ask this because of my trust in Thy great mercy.

If it should please Thy Majesty to send me a suffering
    this day
in exchange for the grace I ask for this soul,
then, it, too, shall please me very much,
and I thank Thee, Most Sweet Jesus,
Shepherd and Lover of Souls;
I thank Thee for this opportunity to give mercy
in thanksgiving for all the mercies
Thou hast shown me. Amen.

A Prayer for the Forgotten Dead

O merciful God,
take pity on those souls
who have no particular friends and intercessors
to recommend them to Thee, who,
either through the negligence of those who are alive,
or through length of time are forgotten
by their friends and by all.
Spare them, O Lord,
and remember Thine own mercy,
when others forget to appeal to it.
Let not the souls which Thou hast created
be parted from thee, their Creator.

May the souls of all the faithful departed,
through the mercy of God, rest in peace. Amen.

A Prayer of Cardinal Newman

O my Lord and Savior,
support me in my last hour

in the strong arms of your sacraments
and by the power of your consolations.
Let the absolving words be said over me.
and the holy oil sign and seal me;
And let Your own Body by my food,
and Your Blood be my sprinkling,
and let my Mother, Mary, breathe on me
and let my angel whisper peace to me.
And my glorious saints and my own
patrons smile upon me that,
In them all and through them all,
I may receive the gift of perseverance
and die as I desire to live —
in your Church,
in your service,
and in your love. Amen.

As cited in *Prayers for Today*, p. 64

A Prayer of Reinhold Niebuhr

O Lord, you have made us very small and we bring our years
to an end like a tale that is told; help us to remember that
beyond our brief day is the eternity of your love.

The Oxford Book of Prayer, no. 543

A Prayer of Saint Thomas More

Give me thy grace, good Lord, to make death no stranger to
me. Give me, good Lord, a longing to be with thee, not for
the avoiding of the calamities of this wretched world; nor
so much for the avoiding of the pains of purgatory, nor the
pains of hell neither, nor so much for the attaining of the
joys of heaven in respect of mine own commodity, as even
for a very love of thee.

The Oxford Book of Prayer, no. 536

A Prayer of Samuel Johnson

O Lord, governor of heaven and earth, in whose hands are embodied and departed spirits, if thou has ordained the souls of the dead to minister to the living, and appointed my departed wife to have care of me, grant that I may enjoy the good effects of her attention and ministration, whether exercised by appearance, impulses, dreams, or in any other manner agreeable to thy government; forgive my presumption, enlighten my ignorance, and however meaner agents are employed, grant me the blessed influences of thy Holy Spirit, through Jesus Christ our Lord.

The Oxford Book of Prayer, no. 540

Notes

1. Susan Sontag, *Illness as Metaphor and AIDS and Its Metaphors* (New York: Picador, 1977, 1989), p. 55.

2. Fred A. Bernstein, "A House Not for Mere Mortals," *The New York Times,* April 3, 2008.

3. Saint Francis of Assisi, *The Hymn of the Sun* (Rhinebeck, NY: Broken Glass/Lancaster Productions, 1990), p. 24. See the complete text on pp. 114–116.

4. Emphasis added. All Mass excerpts are from *The Roman Missal* (International Committee on English in the Liturgy [ICEL], 1973).

5. Lincoln Barnett, *The Universe and Dr. Einstein, with introduction by Albert Einstein* (New York: William Morrow and Company, 1948), p. 106.

6. Ibid.

7. See p. 116.

8. Dag Hammarskjöld, *Markings*, trans. Leif Sjöberg and W. H. Auden (New York: Alfred A. Knopf, 1964), p. 73.

9. "May the great Name of God be exalted and sanctified, throughout the world, which he has created according to his will. May his Kingship be established in your lifetime and in your days, and in the lifetime of the entire household of Israel, swiftly and in the near future; and say, Amen.

"May his great name be blessed, forever and ever. Blessed, praised, glorified, exalted, extolled, honored elevated, and lauded be the Name of the holy one, Blessed is he above and beyond any blessings and hymns, praises and consolations which are uttered in the world; and say, Amen. May there be abundant peace from Heaven, and life, upon us and upon all Israel; and say, Amen. He who makes peace in his high holy places, may he bring peace upon us, and upon all Israel; and say, Amen."

10. Jules Harlow, ed. *A Rabbi's Manual* (New York: Rabbinical Assembly, 1965), p. 130.

11. Byzantine Liturgy.

12. The Office of Christian Burial with Divine Liturgy (Pittsburgh: Byzantine Seminary Press, 1977), p. 18.

13. William J. Whalen, *Separated Brethren, Revised* (Huntington, IN: Our Sunday Visitor, 2002), p. 50.

14. John Wesley, *The Works of the Reverend John Wesley, A.M.* (New York: T. Mason and G. Lane, 1839), p. 401.

15. See *Catechism of the Catholic Church,* n. 1021.

16. *Catherine of Genoa, Purgation and Purgatory, The Spiritual Dialogue,* The Classics of Western Spirituality (New York: Paulist Press, 1979).

17. John Henry Newman, *The Dream of Gerontius,* (New York: St. Paul's/Alba House, 2001).

Sir Edward Elgar, the distinguished English composer, presented his own symphonic poem of "The Dream of Gerontius" in 1900. In 2000 Elgar's work was performed by many of the great symphonies of the world on the occasion of its 100th anniversary.

18. The title can be translated as "A Defense of One's Life." This book was Newman's explanation of his theological views and the reasons for his conversion from Anglicanism to Roman Catholicism.

19. Newman, p. 33.

20. Ibid., p. 36.

21. Ibid., pp. 67–68.

22. Ibid., p. 68.

23. Ibid., p. 71.

24. Pope Benedict XVI, *Spe Salvi*, no. 45.

25. From Pope John Paul II's General Audience of July 28, 1999.

26. See the Epistle to the Romans 1:18-32.

27. From a homily preached by Pope Paul VI on the Solemnity of the Holy Apostles Peter and Paul on Thursday, June 29, 1972.

28. *Spe Salvi*, no. 44.

29. Ibid., no. 46.

30. Philip Schaff and Henry Wace, ed./trans. *A Select Library of Nicene and Post-Nicene Fathers of the Christian Church, Vol. V*, Gregory of Nyssa: Dogmatic Treatises, Etc. (Grand Rapids, MI: Wm. B. Eerdmans Publishing Company) p. 451.

31. Saint Augustine, *The City of God Vol. XVIII–XX*, trans. Gerald G. Walsh, S.J., and Daniel J. Honan (New York: Fathers of the Church, Inc., 1954), pp. 371-372.

32. See Frank J. Sheed, trans., *The Confessions of Saint Augustine* (New York: Sheed & Ward, 1965).

33. *The Confessions of Saint Augustine*, Book IX, 11, 27.

34. See Council of Lyons II (1274): DS 856.

35. See *The Companion to the Catechism of the Catholic Church, Second Edition* (San Francisco: Ignatius Press, 2002), p. 406.

36. See Isaiah 30:33.

37. *Catherine of Genoa*, p. 72.

38. Ibid., p. 73.

39. Ibid., p. 79.

40. See F. X. Schouppe, S.J. *Purgatory Explained by the Lives and Legends of the Saints* (Rockford, IL: Tan Books and Publishers, 1973).

41. See *The Companion to the Catechism of the Catholic Church*, p. 405.

42. *Spe Salvi*, no. 48.

43. James Boswell, *The Life of Samuel Johnson, LL.D., Vol. II* (London: Richardson and Company, 1823), p. 106.

44. Ibid.

45. *Spe Salvi,* no. 47.

46. See Apocalypse 16:12-16.

47. For more information regarding the Final Judgment and the Particular Judgment, see *The Summa Theologica* of Saint Thomas Aquinas, Supplement Question 88.

48. *Spe Salvi*, no. 43.

49. *The Traditional Prayer Book for Sabbath and Festivals*, David de Sola Pool, ed. and trans. (New York: Behrman House, 1960), p. 66.

50. Saint Augustine, Sermon 242a (147), 11: PL 38, 1142.

51. The Paschal Troparion is the great Eastern hymn celebrating Easter.

52. Pope Benedict XVI, *Jesus of Nazareth* (New York: Doubleday, 2007), pp. xi-xxiii.

53. Saint Augustine, *Augustine of Hippo, Selected Writings*, trans. Mary T. Clark, The Classics of Western Spirituality (New York: Paulist Press, 1984), p. 251.

54. Ibid.

55. Saint Augustine, *The City of God Vol. XVIII –XX*, p. 496.

56. Ibid., p. 496.

57. Ibid., p. 497.

58. Ibid., p. 501.

59. Ibid., p. 503.

60. Ibid., p. 504.

61. Ibid.

62. Ibid.

63. Ibid., p. 505.

64. Ibid., p. 506.

65. Ibid.

66. Ibid.

67. Ibid., p. 507.

68. Ibid., p. 508.

69. Ibid., p. 509.

70. Ibid.

71. Ibid., p. 510.

72. *In Paradisum* ("Into Paradise") is an antiphon from the Latin version of the Roman Catholic burial service.

73. From Pope John Paul II's General Audience, Jan. 10, 1990. *L'Osservatore Romano* (Jan. 15, 1990: English edition), p. 3. Italics in original.

BIBLIOGRAPHY

Abrams, M. H., ed. *The Norton Anthology of English Literature, Vol. I.* New York: W. W. Norton & Company, 1968.

Appleton, George, ed. *The Oxford Book of Prayer.* New York: Oxford University Press, 1985.

Augustine. *Augustine of Hippo, Selected Writings.* Translated by Mary T. Clark. The Classics of Western Spirituality. New York: Paulist Press, 1984.

———. *The City of God, Vol. XVIII –XX.* Translated by Gerald G. Walsh, S.J., and Daniel J. Honan. New York: Fathers of the Church Inc., 1954.

———.*The Confessions of Saint Augustine.* Translated by Frank J. Sheed. New York: Sheed & Ward, 1965.

Barnett, Lincoln. *The Universe and Dr. Einstein,* New York: William Morrow and Company, 1948.

Benedict XVI. *Jesus of Nazareth.* New York: Doubleday, 2007.

Boswell, James. *The Life of Samuel Johnson, Vol. II.* London: Richardson and Company, 1823.

Excerpts from *Catherine of Genoa: Purgation and Purgatory, The Spiritual Dialogue,* translated by Serge Hughes. Copyright © 1979 by The Missionary Society of St. Paul the Apostle in the State of New York. Paulist Press: New York/Mahwah, NJ. Reprinted by permission of Paulist Press, Inc., *www.paulistpress.com.*

Community of Saint Mary, Eastern Province, ed. *The Monastic Diurnal Revised.* Peekskill, New York: The Community of Saint Mary, 1989.

The Companion to the Catechism of the Catholic Church, Second Edition. San Francisco: Ignatius Press, 2002.

Cooke, Terence. *Prayers for Today.* New York: Alba House, 1991.

Epstein, Isidore. *Judaism.* New York: Penguin Books, 1959.

Ferguson, Margaret, et al., eds. *The Norton Anthology of Poetry.* New York: W.W. Norton & Company, 1970.

Francis of Assisi. *The Hymn of the Sun*. Rhinebeck, New York: Broken Glass/Lancaster Productions, 1990.

Gillman, Neil. *The Death of Death*. Woodstock, Vermont: Jewish Lights Publishing, 1997.

Gregory of Nyssa. *A Select Library of Nicene and Post-Nicene Fathers of the Christian Church, Vol. V, Gregory of Nyssa: Dogmatic Treatises, etc.* Edited/translated by Philip Schaff and Henry Wace, Grand Rapids, Michigan: Wm. B. Eerdmans Publishing Company.

Hammarskjöld, Dag. *Markings*. Translated by Leif Sjöberg and W. H. Auden. New York: Alfred A. Knopf, 1964.

Hapgood, Isabel Florence, ed./trans. *Service Book of the Holy Orthodox-Catholic Apostolic Church*. Englewood, New Jersey: Antiochian Orthodox Christian Archdiocese of North America, 1996.

Harlow, Jules, ed. *A Rabbi's Manual*. New York: Rabbinical Assembly, 1965.

Heschel, Abraham Joshua. *Moral Grandeur and Spiritual Audacity*. Edited by Susannah Heschel. New York: Farrar, Straus and Giroux, 1996.

John Paul II. *Prayers and Meditations*. Edited by Bishop Peter Canisius Johnannes van Lierde, O.S.A. New York: Penguin Books, 1984.

Johnson, Thomas H., ed. *The Complete Poems of Emily Dickinson*. Boston: Little Brown and Company, 1960.

Kipling, Rudyard. *Rudyard Kipling's Verse: Definitive Edition*. New York: Doubleday and Company, 1940.

Lindsay, Vachel. *Collected Poems of Vachel Lindsay*. New York: Macmillan Publishing Company, 1925.

Newman, John Henry. *The Dream of Gerontius*. New York: St. Paul's/Alba House, 2001.

————. *The Heart of Newman*. San Francisco: Ignatius Press, 1997.

————. *Prayers, Verses, and Devotions*. San Francisco: Ignatius Press, 1989.

O'Connor, James T. *Land of the Living*. New York: Catholic Book Publishing Company, 1992.

Pool, David de Sola, ed./trans. *The Traditional Prayer Book for Sabbath and Festivals.* New York: Behrman House, 1960.

Quiller-Couch, Sir Arthur, ed. *The Oxford Book of English Verse: 1250-1918.* New York: Oxford University Press, 1972.

Rahner, Karl. *Prayers for a Lifetime.* Edited by Albert Raffelt. New York: Crossroad, 1995.

The Roman Missal. International Committee on English in the Liturgy (ICEL), 1973.

Schouppe, F. X. *Purgatory Explained by the Lives and Legends of the Saints.* Rockford, Illinois: Tan Books and Publishers, 1973.

Sontag, Susan. *Illness as Metaphor and AIDS and Its Metaphors.* New York: Picador, 1977, 1989.

Tolstoy, Leo. *The Great Short Works of Leo Tolstoy.* Translated by Louise and Aylmer Maude. New York: Harper & Row, 1967.

The Union Prayerbook. New York: Central Conference of American Rabbis, 1945.

Walsh, Thomas, ed. *The Catholic Anthology: The World's Great Catholic Poetry.* New York: The Macmillan Company, 1947.

Ware, Timothy. *The Orthodox Church.* New York: Penguin Books, 1963.

Wesley, John. *The Works of the Reverend John Wesley, A.M.* New York: T. Mason and G. Lane, 1839.

Whalen, William J. *Separated Brethren, Revised.* Huntington, Indiana: Our Sunday Visitor, 2002.

Papal documents not cited above or in the notes are taken from the Vatican website, *www.vatican.va*.